LEAN SUPPLY CHAIN

COLLECTED PRACTICES AND CASES

PRODUCTIVITY PRESS

New York, New York

Most Productivity Press books are available at quantity discounts when purchased in bulk. For more information contact our Customer Service Department (888-319-5852). Address all other inquiries to:

Productivity Press
444 Park Avenue South, 7th floor
New York, NY 10016
United States of America
Telephone: 212-686-5900
Fax: 212-686-5411
E-mail: info@productivitypress.com

Material originally appeared in the *Lean Manufacturing Advisor*, 1999-2005.

Library of Congress Cataloging-in-Publication Data
Lean supply chain : collected practices & cases.
        p. cm. — (Insights on implementation)
"Material originally appeared in The Lean Manufacturing Advisor, 1999-2005."
Includes bibliographical references and index.
ISBN 1-56327-330-6 (alk. paper)
1. Business logistics–Case studies. 2. Industrial management–Case studies. 3. Industrial efficiency–Case studies. I. Productivity Press. II. Lean manufacturing advisor. III. Series.
  HD38.5.L434 2005
  658.7–dc22

                                                                2005028683

08 07   9 8 7 6 5 4 3 2

Contents

Chapter 9

Chapter 10

Chapter 11

Chapter 12

Chapter 13

Chapter 14

Part III: Improving Distribution

Chapter 15

Chapter 16

Chapter 17

Chapter 18

Chapter 19

Introduction

A complete value stream extends beyond the four walls of your enterprise. It includes suppliers who provide you with parts and raw materials, as well as customers who purchase your finished goods. Therefore, any lean transformation that does not, at some point, focus on the extended supply chain is fundamentally incomplete.

However, transforming your supply chain is not easy. Much of what takes place outside your factory is not under your control. You may not even have access to the information needed to completely map the flow of goods. Supply chain initiatives require not only a thorough understanding of lean principles and skill to apply those principles, but close working relationships with suppliers and customers, where they become true partners working with you to implement strategy.

How to tackle the thorny issues of supply chain transformation has been the focus of many articles in Lean Manufacturing Advisor, a newsletter that each month chronicles how companies are implementing lean principles. Many of the articles, which originally appeared in the newsletter over several years, are case studies of companies addressing supply chain challenges. We bring together these articles in the book you now hold in your hands.

---

[1] For more information regarding the articles in this book, including the original dates of publication, please refer to the citations section.

The first section of this book looks at the broad strategy issues involved in making your supply chain lean. The chapters of the second session chronicle efforts to meet the challenges involved in building supply chain partnerships with both suppliers and customers. Finally, some nuts-and-bolts approaches to improving distribution are described in the chapters of the third section.

This book is a unique compilation of stories from the front lines – supply and distribution lines – of the lean revolution. We hope the case studies and advice contained in these stories will provide valuable insights you can apply as you implement your own initiatives.

Ralph Bernstein
Editor
Lean Manufacturing Advisor

Part I
Supply Chain Strategies

OVERVIEW

As with improvement efforts that occur on the shop floor, efforts to improve the supply chain should not be approached piecemeal. Ideally, you should have a broad understanding of your supply chain and develop a strategy for its transformation. The chapters in this section focus on creating and implementing such a strategy.

Of course, addressing supply chain issues is not the first step you take in a lean transformation; you need to get your own house in order first. But how do you know when you are ready to tackle the supply chain? Chapter One, originally published as a Lean Advisor Q&A column, provides an answer.

For a global corporation that manufactures and sells a broad array of products worldwide, the supply chain is incredibly complicated. Chapter Two describes the efforts of Delphi Corporation to identify and reduce the complexity of its supply chain.

For shoe manufacturer adidas, time to market is a more significant issue than complexity. How the company is improving supply chain operations to cut its time to market in half is the focus of Chapter Three.

The global supply chain of the U.S. military is just as a complex as with Delphi or adidas. Chapter Four, originally published after the U.S. launched operations in Afghanistan (but before the invasion of Iraq), describes a shift in American strategy aimed at keeping troops better supplied.

And Chapter Five describes a follow-up study by the RAND Corporation on the results of those efforts in Afghanistan, comparing logistics there to those of military operations in other parts of the world.

Expanding an Initiative Beyond Your Enterprise

November, 2002

When is the right time to do lean supply chain?

As with any of the keys to improvement in the Lean Management System, Supply Chain Development has a position in the sequence of initiatives. The debate about this particular dynamic of the lean effort seems to be centered on "when" is the proper time. (Of course, critical/survival issues in the supply chain must be dealt with as they occur and need no analysis to be made visible.)

It would be an oversimplification to answer this question by saying, "You are ready for this phase when the gap analysis indicates it as the next important opportunity for improvement." "But what are the business conditions when that will happen?" is the retort.

Here are some conditions to look for. You are ready for Supply Chain Development when:

- The production plan has 80-85% execution accuracy on a weekly basis. In other words, your build-to-schedule measurement is in that range. This will allow you to give your suppliers an accurate look at your short-term needs with a low probability of change.

- Your inventory accuracy is greater than 95% on a cycle-counted basis. Your requirements will be more accurate since parts will not be lost/found in the system.

- You have used production-smoothing techniques (inventory buffering, kanban, heijunka boxes, etc.) where they are needed — and they are effective.

- You have an effective and accurate supplier rating system that is used to monitor performance.

- If one of the major sources of variation in the value stream can be traced to the supply chain, it's time.

Remember, you must deal with critical supply problems on a case-by-case basis, but when managing the supply chain as one of the dynamics in the business, you will need a system.

TAKEAWAYS

- Only begin lean supply chain when production execution accuracy and inventory accuracy are both high.
- Know how to rate your suppliers and monitor their performance.
- Be seeking to address variation in the supply chain.

2

Reducing Supply Chain Complexity

April, 2002

Long accustomed to mapping the value streams within factories for the products they make, executives at Delphi Automotive Systems decided to extend their efforts beyond the factory walls. They sought to identify every step involved in getting a product to a customer, including not just manufacturing processes but every action in the supply chain as well.

Delphi is a global company with about 200 manufacturing sites and roughly 200,000 employees – so it's not surprising that getting a product to a customer is a complex process.

Too complex, executives found.

"It takes 171 organizations and a total of 288 handoffs just to bring the product to the customer," said Mark Lorenz, vice president of operations and logistics.

Lorenz — speaking at a conference sponsored by The Management Roundtable in Dallas – was describing the steps connected with just one product, which he did not identify. But he did say that Delphi applied lean principles to simplify and streamline all that complexity.

In the case of that particular product, the number of organizations involved (both inside and outside Delphi) has been reduced to 73,

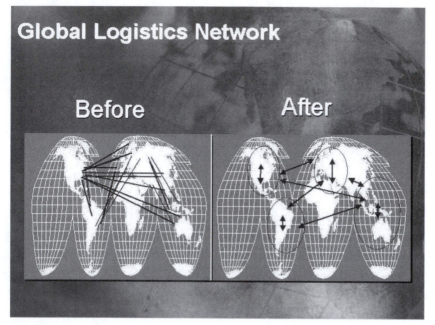

By reconfiguring its Global Logistics Network, Delphi significantly reduced the numbers of freight forwarders and ocean carriers.

and now there are only 82 handoffs. "We're still thinking that's too many," Lorenz said.

In addition, the production process has been streamlined so that only one plant is involved instead of two – which has the added benefit of freeing up capacity in the plant no longer involved.

The achievement with that product's delivery is part of a much larger picture at Delphi, where the implementation of lean manufacturing has been expanded to include streamlining the supply chain.

The approaches taken include working on rates, forming partnerships with supply chain companies, route modeling, and reducing the number of locations involved as well as the number of shippers. In addition, "we've eliminated probably 40 to 50 percent of our warehouses, and there are more to take out," Lorenz explained.

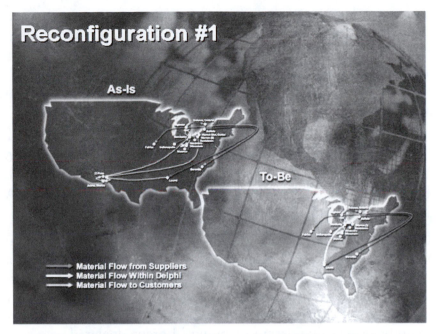

The distances products must be transported are cut by reducing the number of organizations and the number of handoffs in product flow, and from better route mapping.

The result so far, he said, is that Delphi's total logistics costs – including transportation, customs and duties, freight expenses, and warehousing – have been cut to about 2.5 percent of revenues, down from a range of five to six percent. "We feel that's a benchmark," Lorenz declared.

A Major Challenge

Delphi began its lean journey in 1996 and is recognized today as a leader in implementing lean processes. Five of its plants were 2002 winners of the Shingo Prize for Excellence in Manufacturing.

Addressing supply chain issues is a big job for Delphi, given the scope of its operations. The company produces more than 130 product lines; Lorenz jokingly referred to Delphi as "the Wal-Mart of automotive companies," with products for dynamics and propulsion, electronics and mobile communication, and safety, thermal and electrical architecture. Each day, Delphi ships eight million parts with 150,000 part numbers to more than 100 customers. In a lighthearted comparison, Lorenz stated that Burger King sells approximately seven million hamburgers a day with about six part numbers.

He also offered a supply chain comparison. Three major airports – Chicago, Los Angeles and Dallas – are responsible for 2,846 flights, or ship windows, per day, Lorenz said, while Delphi handles 3,000 shipments per day – which are 99 percent on time. A diagram of Delphi's logistics literally covers the globe.

To make its manufacturing lean, Delphi created the Delphi Manufacturing System, modeled after the renowned Toyota Production System. For its supply chain, Delphi has established its Global Logistics Network and has been striving to streamline every aspect of that network. "We are compressing the size of the supply chain by using value stream mapping," Lorenz declared.

Product flow to customers has been realigned so that shipments rarely, rather than regularly, travel from one continent to another.

Delphi used to work with 35 freight forwarders and 56 ocean carriers. Now it has three global LMCs and 12 ocean carriers; Lorenz says the company would like to reduce that latter figure to nine.

It's Information That Counts

However, the real challenge in transforming the supply chain was information flow. "If you don't have good information flow, material flow is just expediting," Lorenz commented.

Toward that end, Delphi and technology partner Covisint created a supplier portal – a Web page that "helped us eliminate the complexity we had with multi-division communication" between Delphi and its more than 5,000 global suppliers, he said.

"The supplier portal also supports our vision for electronically linking our supply chain. Through this portal, we expect to improve customer service and improve our ability to achieve cost reductions," he added. The portal is designed to help streamline procurement, production and shipping.

For example, Lorenz notes that even third-tier suppliers can get information through the portal, which gives them a much earlier indication of likely orders. "The old way, the third-tier supplier may not have seen that for four weeks out," Lorenz states.

In addition, Delphi is using a Covisint tool called Inventory Visibility that monitors min/max information.

"We are using information through the portal to forecast where demand is going the next four or five weeks. We are able to smooth out ripples in our own manufacturing," Lorenz said.

Delphi also offers electronic messaging for suppliers for two-way communication.

In addressing supply chain issues, Delphi has not abandoned its focus on eliminating waste from its manufacturing operations. Continuous flow, small lot production strategy, elimination of waste, improvements in quality and the other principles of lean manufacturing are still embodied in the Delphi Manufacturing System, which remains the company standard.

For the future, Delphi remains absolutely committed to continuing its lean journey, Lorenz stressed, even at a time when world problems can threaten supply chain disruptions.

"We have no plans to change our lean philosophy or practices," he said. "Carrying excess inventory is an unnecessary expense."

TAKEAWAYS

- Mapping the supply chain is essential.
- Supply chains can be improved by reducing the numbers of organizations involved, handoffs and warehouses.
- Smooth information flow is critical.

3

In a Race Against Time, adidas Leaps Forward

October, 2002

An athlete may use a pair of adidas shoes to increase his running speed. As part of a global initiative, adidas is using lean manufacturing to increase how quickly those shoes get to the athlete.

The company makes a broad spectrum of footwear, apparel and accessories at more than 500 factories in 63 countries. Designing, manufacturing and distributing those products takes careful planning, large-scale production, and complex logistics — and it takes time.

That's the problem. If adidas takes too much time to spot and respond to changing consumer preferences — not to mention manufacture the products — it may miss sales opportunities and/or find itself stuck with footwear nobody wants.

That's why adidas is now targeting a 50 percent reduction in time-to-market every year. And that's why the company is more than two years into a lean manufacturing initiative designed to help achieve that goal.

It's an effort that already is starting to bear fruit. It used to take 90 days from an initial request for a product to having it delivered. Today, in many cases, it takes only 60 days, according to David Freni, head of strategic planning — global operations for adidas

At a massive factory complex in Guangdong, China, tens of thousands of employees making adidas shoes have shifted from batch-and-queue processes to continuous flow operations.

International. That broad improvement results from an accumulation of gains in a variety of areas, including dock-to-dock time within factories, "cut-to-box" time, and accuracy, meaning having products built on time, packaged and delivered in accordance with the original plan.

The 30-day reduction can make a big difference. "If we have 30 days more to delay the actual commitment of, let's say, the sizes of a particular color of a particular product, the decision-making process of choosing the correct product improves anywhere from 25 to 55 percent," Freni says. "What we're seeing is two things: one is that our customer is ordering the correct thing, more accuracy in terms of size and color, and we're getting larger orders as well. They're less risk-averse, willing to commit to more production."

Freni believes this will ultimately produce both greater sales for adidas and fewer markdowns, with improvements of up to 20 percent in each of those two areas, or a total "window of opportunity" of as much as 40 percent. It will take several more seasons to see the results, he adds, noting that a "season" in the footwear industry lasts about six months.

In August, parent company adidas-Salomon announced a net sales increase of 10 percent in the second quarter. Operating expenses were 40.2 percent of sales, up 0.4 percentage points. However, inventories were down 12 percent from a year earlier, and receivables were up 4 percent (which was less than sales growth). Net debt decreased 10 percent, the biggest year-over-year debt reduction since the Salomon acquisition.

The time-to-market initiative involves a coordinated, global effort on the part of adidas and its consultants. A major part of that effort has been training that leads to lean implementations in factories around the world. The effort also involves technology improvements in supply chain planning, and it is beginning to focus on the company's internal design process.

Transforming Factories Worldwide

adidas outsources most of its manufacturing; the vast majority of factories that make adidas products are owned by other companies. But those companies — nearly 60 of them — are jumping on the adidas lean bandwagon "because of adidas' influence and the amount of capacity they consumed at these factories," notes Fred Flynn, one of several consultants with Productivity, Inc., who worked with adidas for more than four years.

"adidas is probably the first company I'm aware of that has taken on such a large responsibility for education of their tier one suppliers," Flynn adds.

It's a daunting task, not only because of the number of factories involved, but also because of the size of some operations. One of the largest is a vast complex in Guangdong, China, employing nearly 90,000 people. A second complex nearby employs another 20,000.

Operations were traditional batch-and-queue. For example, a five-story building at the site was divided up by process. Cutting of raw materials occurred in batches on the first floor. The cut pieces were bundled and sent to storage in a warehouse, then brought back several days later for preparation on another floor. More warehouse storage would follow, until the prepared materials were brought back for sewing on still another floor.

In China, and everywhere else the consultants went, training has been a critical part of the transformation. Several dozen managers at a time went through a four-week training program. That was followed by the consultants working with the graduates to transform the shop floor, creating manufacturing cells. Visual controls have also been established in many operations.

Results vary among factories, but the benefits are clear. Work in process was reduced by amounts ranging from 54 percent to 98 percent, Flynn says, while lead times went down from 25 percent to 97 percent. Improvements in productivity — pairs per person per hour — also covered a broad range, but averaged about 50 percent, he adds.

Initially, all the efforts focused on footwear factories. More recently, the initiative has expanded to include apparel factories, which tend to be smaller but are greater in number. Lean efforts were launched not only in China, but also at factories in Taiwan, Istanbul, Tunisia, Vietnam, Indonesia, the Philippines, Bulgaria and Turkey.

Doing It Right

"The training is fundamental," Freni says. "You can relate the success in the factory directly to how well you've trained not only senior management people, but down in the factory too. They have to understand how they contribute to the overall picture, and what the overall picture is. If you spend the time up front doing that, then they become part of the solution."

The other key factor, he states, is establishing a baseline, "understanding where you're at before you start changing things, so you understand how you've changed things, and how much.

"Those two things are pretty much the core of getting it right. If you do those two things well, eventually the shop floor is pushing this and setting new limits. Then you really have a lean environment."

Stanley Mao is coordinator of lean manufacturing for Apache Footwear in Guangdong, a manufacturer for adidas. In an e-mail reply to questions about the lean transformation, he commented that "it was very difficult to get our employees involved in lean implementation, due to the fact that they didn't know what lean was ... Therefore, we established a training program to train our supervisors first to let them understand the lean principles and change their thoughts and minds in different stages. Furthermore, these supervisors (key trainers) were responsible for training their employees step by step to ensure everyone really understands and accepts lean principles."

Mao also said benefits at his factory include "freeing up floor space, reduced staffing needs and shortened production cycles. By running one-pair flow in stitching and assembly, WIP has been reduced by about 30 percent."

Flynn praises adidas for developing a productive working relationship with the consultants. "They did it right," he says. "The steps they took were the proper steps." These included educating the consultants about the footwear and apparel business, so that the consultants could customize training materials for the factories.

He also stresses that adidas followed a traditional — and worthwhile — direction in its efforts. "The first place you always go is into manufacturing," he explains. "Because adidas doesn't have manufacturing, they went to the supplier base. That's the same thing anybody would do, even in a small manufacturing operation. You look at the total value stream. Manufacturing is the first place you go. Now they are starting to work internally. Now their design time is longer than their manufacturing lead time."

Freni confirms that "we're hoping in 2003 we can begin to address the product creation process." Some processes have been re-engineered throughout the supply chain, to facilitate rapid prototyping, for example.

An Ongoing Initiative

Freni notes that adidas has also been developing new computer planning systems. "They've allowed us to plan the factories more effectively," he states. "We think that through the use of the system we'll be able to plan three to four percent more production in the month it is requested." Actions have included linking customers to central planning operations and moves to forge better links with material suppliers.

adidas has also established a website specific to lean. There are chat rooms, and best practices are posted.

In hindsight, Freni believes it would have been helpful early on to have translated more materials into local languages. He also believes in avoiding information overload: "You should give sufficient information, but not more than is needed at various levels. Try to simplify it so people get very good at the portion they have to understand, but do not get burdened with, let's say, theoretical aspects."

The initiative is an ongoing effort, and far from mature. Freni notes that, currently, "we're hoping to stabilize the 60-day timeline. That's really more an issue of getting the rest of the supply chain on the sales side to adjust to the paradigm." Flynn notes that adidas is also starting to look at working with its tier two suppliers.

Beyond achieving the goal of a reduced time-to-market, Freni sees another gain: "The principal benefit both for us and the factories is we have gotten to understand one another much better. We have clear measurables and can communicate in a common language, a lean language. And because we as a brand are initiating this training, reaching out to our supply chain partners, we are building a bond that historically has not been a traditional one. A lot of that is built on mutual understanding and clear measurements."

TAKEAWAYS

- Supply chain improvement is one way to improve time to market.
- A large manufacturer can take the lead in educating suppliers.
- Having the right relationship with consultants can be valuable.

4

A New Paradigm Supports U.S. Troops

September, 2002

As American soldiers fought terrorism in Afghanistan, a subtle but significant change occurred in the Army's operations.

When soldiers first arrived in November 2001, the military supplied them in much the same way it had supported past military operations: by shipping the supplies its leaders thought would be required, and storing them nearby — in this case, in Uzbekistan.

That matched the way things were done in 1991 during Operation Desert Storm. At that time, "we hauled 60 to 90 days worth of consumption into Saudi Arabia and stacked it in gigantic piles," notes Tom Edwards, deputy to the commanding general of the U.S. Army Combined Arms Support Command, based in Fort Lee, Va.

But in June of 2002, the First Corps Support Command — the military logistics agency supporting Operation Enduring Freedom — began to put new procedures in place. These involved storing fewer supplies on site, and shipping only what the troops actually said they needed.

Colonel Sue Wagner, a leader of the new Uzbekistan supply operation, says her crew officially took over on July 8th. Less than a month later, she says, "we had already identified $10 million in excess material" that had been delivered. At least half of that is likely to be shipped back, she adds.

Soldiers load ammunition onto a waiting CH-47 Chinook helicopter, which delivers the cargo to troops fighting in the mountains near Gardez, Afghanistan.

The change in supply practices was not made up on the spot. It was the culmination of a seven-year effort to transform U.S. military logistics — a paradigm shift from a supply-driven system to a pull distribution system.

Working with the nonprofit RAND institution, the Army has developed a wide range of new rules and procedures, streamlined many practices, and begun using data from management information systems for a new hierarchy of linked metrics (see diagram, p.22).

Even before June, the years of effort were bearing fruit in the current operation. According to Dr. John Dumond, director of the Military Logistics Program for RAND, customer wait time (CWT) — the period from a customer ordering an item until the order is filled — was ranging from 12 to 17 days in Uzbekistan in the early months of this year. "In the past, the military would have ordered large amounts of stock and waited a long time for it to show up — easily 30, 40, or 50 days," Dumond says. "If you see what we're doing these days — 15 days — and think about how far an advance that is, that's pretty extraordinary."

The overall initiative — called Velocity Management — is a powerful example of how the principles of lean manufacturing can be applied to logistics and distribution, eliminating waste and gaining widespread supply chain efficiencies.

The new practices have been or are being implemented at bases throughout the world, and are also gaining some attention from other branches of the armed forces. As a result of the effort, "key Army logistics processes have improved dramatically on the three dimensions of performance: time, quality and cost," according to a RAND report published in 2001.

In addition, troops in an actual military campaign, such as Afghanistan, not only receive supplies faster, but also face a greatly reduced burden of storing and protecting those supplies.

Gigantic Inefficiency

In the early 1990s, the RAND report says, the Army's logistics system was "unreliable, inefficient, unresponsive to changing customer needs and expensive."

Concerns over the problems led to the Velocity Management initiative, launched in 1995. One of the first efforts of that drive was to establish baseline measurements, using the year ending June 30, 1995. That revealed that the average customer wait time was almost a month, that CWT performance was highly variable, and that this slow and variable performance was present in all segments of the logistics process.

Most Army logistics efforts are aimed at supplying established locations, such as military bases. But concerns over the delays and uncertainties of shipments meant that whenever a military operation was launched, commanders would stockpile huge quantities of supplies on scene to reduce the risk of running out.

During the first three months of the Gulf War, the RAND report observes, more than one million tons of supplies and equipment

The Goal Is to Move from This . . .

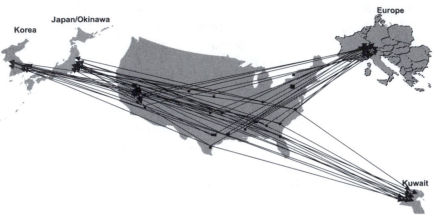

A system that was not well rationalized —

. . . To This

A Strategic Defense Distribution System
Integrated and Synchronized for Global Performance

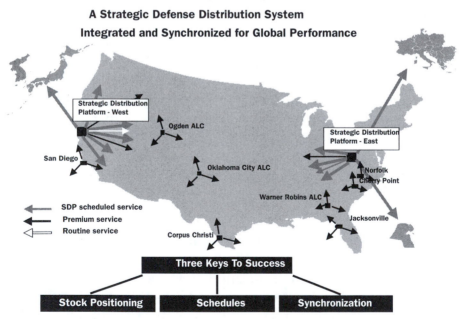

were shipped to the combat region, with another 175,000 tons airlifted in.

To implement the VM system, the Army institutionalized an improvement method called DMI — Define, Measure, Improve. Dumond compares it to change management approaches in the private sector, such as Toyota's Plan-Do-Check-Act methodology.

VM has been implemented by two types of teams. Army-wide Process Improvement Teams (PITs) consist of a variety of technical experts and seek to define their respective processes, develop process-wide metrics and performance reports, analyze performance and recommend changes. Site Improvement Teams (SITs) are installation-level teams of local technical experts and managers who apply DMI to local processes and implement Army-wide improvements.

The processes for repairing equipment and providing spare parts have been a significant focus of VM.

The Right Measurements

From the beginning, development of new metrics has been a critical part of the initiative. End-to-end customer wait time — which measures how long it takes to place an order, how long before the item is available, and how long it takes to ship it to the customer — was not measured before VM.

The Army did apply metrics to its logistics processes. But as the RAND report notes, "members of the VM teams found that many segments of the process were being managed with metrics that focused on local effectiveness or efficiency but did not necessarily result in good customer service. For example, in some segments of the process, organizations measured themselves by the efficient use of trucks, with the result that partial truckloads were held up until a full one could be assembled. While this goal and this metric yielded more efficient use of trucks, for many orders it delayed getting the needed part to the customer."

Edwards offers another example: "In automated systems that are batch-driven, a material release order is processed by the depot man-

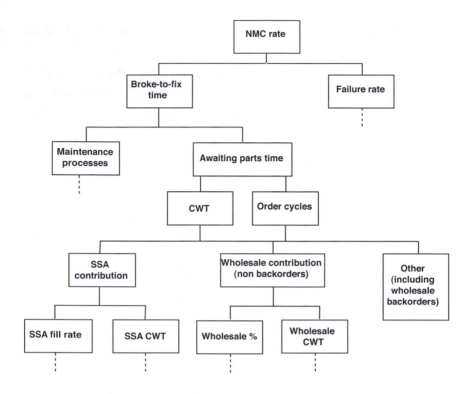

The Army created an Equipment Downtime Analyzer (EDA) that uses data from information systems to create a hierarchy of linked metrics. NMC = Not Mission Capable. CWT = Customer Wait Time. SSA = Supply Support Activity.

agement system. It's put in a bin to be pulled down by the depot system, picked and packed. Inventory management stopped the clock (on measuring process time) when they put the order in the bin. The depots would only pull down things out of the bin once a day. The mean time (before an order was pulled out of the bin) was about 12 hours. That's 12 hours in the process that nobody owns. That's perpetuated every time there's a batch process that's an intermediary."

In these situations, he said, the improvement team would allocate the "dead time" to one side or the other. "Taking out those unowned slack times was worth about five days," Edwards boasts.

Because CWT was so variable, the CWT team developed a new suite of metrics: 50th percentile, meaning the time by which half the ordered items arrive (median CWT), plus 75th and 95th percentile CWTs. The latter two metrics help identify the orders that take the longest time to be filled and delivered.

But CWT was not the only metric developed. Some others are:

- Equipment readiness — the percentage of weapon systems that are operational.

- Fill rate — the percentage of customer requests that are immediately filled from a given inventory point.

- Accommodation rate — the percentage of requisitions for items regularly stocked, whether or not the requested item is available at the time of the request. This measures inventory "breadth."

- Satisfaction rate — the percentage of accommodated requests for which there is stock available at the time of the request. This measures inventory "depth."

Broad Deployment

To achieve performance improvements, the VM teams applied the Define-Measure-Improve process — and lean principles — to a wide range of operations, including:

Shipping: Army installations strengthened oversight, simplified rules, improved the performance of new requisitioning and receipting technologies and increased their proper use, reduced review processes and streamlined on-post delivery.

Some problems were caused by the use of a wide range of shipping modes, which could cause delays when mixed. To solve the problem, the Army established regularly scheduled truck runs as the primary shipping mode to large installations. Many routes between supply depots and installations could be traveled in a day or two days, and volume was large enough to justify sending a truck daily or every other day.

25

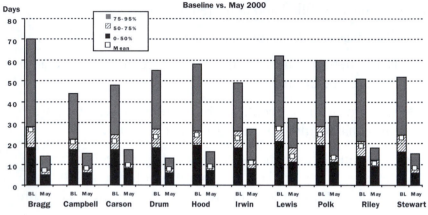

**All Major US Army Installations
Made Substantial Progress**

Order & Ship Times (orders for repair parts, no backorders)

Baseline vs. May 2000

Source: RAND

To help make it work, the Defense Logistics Agency (DLA) began using automation to sort packages into multi-packs that streamlined the shipment and receipt of multiple items to a single installation, and to specific locations on that installation.

In addition, DLA changed the stock positions at some depots to better match the needs of the installations served by those depots (see Inventory section below).

DLA also increased the use of automated, scannable manifest cards for major customers on Army installations, reducing the time and effort needed to receive shipments and produce receipts.

Meanwhile, the installations redesigned delivery routes to be more efficient. Officers also improved the training of supply clerks on using automated receipting tools and worked with the supplier to improve their design and operability. Staffers were given new work schedules so they could meet scheduled trucks at the right time and place. They redesigned on-post distribution systems so shipments that were received were more quickly distributed internally.

Inventory: RAND analysts improved the algorithms used to calculate which items to stock, and how much of each. These changes were designed to take into account the cost of an item, its mobility (meaning whether it could be stored in the 90-inch containers used to deploy most stocks), its demand pattern, and transition costs. This last point refers to the fact that an Army unit may not have enough funds to make all recommended changes to inventory, making inventory improvement a continuous process.

These new algorithms were used first to increase inventory breadth. Substantial numbers of items were added to supply depot inventories, but primarily inexpensive items. This improved the fill rate because mechanics obtained more of what they needed, and that improved customer wait time. Many of these low-cost items are small; space was created for them by removing items no longer in demand and by decreasing quantities of items with little demand. Thus, total weight and volume increased only marginally, or declined. Plus, warehouses and containers were reconfigured to use space more efficiently.

Depth of inventory — the quantities stocked — was also improved. Buffer stocks were reduced because CWT had improved, meaning replacement stocks could be obtained more quickly.

In addition, depth was adjusted for those items with "lumpy" demand. Since having enough stock to cover spikes in demand could be expensive, the new algorithms permit adjustment of targeted service levels. For inexpensive items, the goal might be to fill an order in one or two days; for more expensive items, it might be longer.

A depot in Susquehanna, Pa., is an example of how the system was improved, according to Edwards. The depot's practice was to fill high-priority orders in one day, with up to four days allowed for more routine orders. Demand was uneven; the depot might have 27,000 orders on Monday or Tuesday, and 11,000 on Wednesday or Thursday. "Using this four-day rule to level the workload, they would push off routine orders from Monday to Wednesday or Thursday. The net result was that everything that's four day gets pushed to the fourth day," Edwards explains.

"The lesson we learned from looking at lean practices," he goes on, "is to do today's work today." Depot commanders said it couldn't be done, but adjustments to the system made it possible. "Now not only do we fill all orders in one day, but all receipts are done in one day," Edwards says. "That's all due to metrics: one-day order entry, one-day receipt take-up."

The vast majority of nearly 150 Army warehouses have implemented at least some of the new algorithms, with significant increases in fill rates, according to RAND.

Repairs: The Army defined repair cycle time (RCT) as the time from an item being reported broken to the time it is repaired and made available for use. But an improvement team found that Army data systems were not designed to measure the full repair cycle — a problem that RAND analysts found could be solved by combining information from a number of data systems. Doing so revealed that repair cycle time "was much too long and variable, both for components and end items," the RAND report states. In 1996, the Army set a goal of reducing RCT by 50 percent.

Study of repair processes led to a variety of changes, including reducing the administrative workload on maintenance personnel so they could spend more time on repairs; eliminating repetitive inspections, with the remaining inspections linked to specific technical requirements, and eliminating unnecessary cleaning procedures.

By 1998, in one typical example, the average RCT at a major Army installation had decreased 38 percent at the 75th percentile, without any increase in staffing or other resources. In fact, commanders reported reductions in the repair workload and in backlogs.

Better Information

The teams also targeted improvements in technology and information flow.

Financial information is one area. The teams found that price and credit information was frequently poor and untimely, requiring financial checks at many levels to ensure funds are available before requisitions are released.

The changes needed require high-level decisions across various divisions. The RAND report states that "a continued commitment from Army leadership is required to secure cooperation across functional stovepipes both within and outside the Army and to secure the funding needed."

Another Army goal is to improve equipment readiness. The VM initiative led to development of the Equipment Downtime Analyzer (EDA), a relational database that saves, integrates and analyzes data already collected. It determines how much each process and organization contributes to equipment downtime, producing metrics that describe equipment failure rates and the "broke-to-fix" process.

The RAND report said the EDA holds great promise and is "targeted for integration into the first release of the Army's new management information system for logistics."

Information technology is also proving critical in the new pull system in Uzbekistan, according to Brigadier General Ann Dunwoody, who heads the First Corps Support Command. Radio-frequency tags and scanners as well as computer workstations with secure e-mail accounts are all part of the picture.

When the new effort began in June 2002, "we started getting a handle on what was coming through the pipeline — rations, for instance," she explains. "We started tracking by sea, rail and ship. We were able to turn off some of that stuff that we knew wasn't required. We need one central fusion cell that has visibility as to what the requirements are, and the ability to move things around. It has allowed us to review our stocking objectives and then adjust."

But technology is only the enabler, the general adds. Other elements are organizational change and cultural change; on the latter point, "we work that every day. You have to give people confidence that you don't need to keep pushing stuff."

Edwards and Dumond stress the importance of top leadership commitment to make the change happen. Dumond says that "the Army leadership was ready for that change, so they embraced the idea that having a 25-day wait time for parts was too long. The very senior logistics generals of the Army got together and made that choice. Once the generals got on board, the rest follow."

Supporting the Troops

Uzbekistan may be the first operation in a military deployment putting the emphasis on a pull system, but it's not the first time the Army has seen combat-region benefits from the initiative. The RAND report notes that shipments to troops deployed to Bosnia and Kosovo achieved the same lower levels in customer wait time, compared to the 1995 baseline, as military bases and other locations.

In Uzbekistan, Dunwoody describes the support operation as being in an "evolutionary stage."

"We will continue to improve upon the capability at all distribution hubs," she states. We're not there yet. We have to work harder to discipline ourselves about using technology. Communication continues to improve every day."

And how will the new processes be deployed in future military operations — for example, if the United States invades Iraq?

"I would think this capability should be the first in," Dunwoody says. "That did not happen in this case (Uzbekistan). I hope we have lessons learned, and this would be the way to go."

TAKEAWAYS

- Baseline measurements are required as a starting point.
- New metrics must often be developed for a supply chain initiative.
- Improving flow of information about many areas, not just shipping (such as pricing) can help speed orders and deliveries.

5

Report: Lean Afghan Logistics Were Better Than Desert Storm

June, 2004

During the first three months of U.S. military operations in Afghanistan (October-December 2001), defense agencies were able to supply the troops there with the support they needed, primarily because implementation of lean strategies improved defense logistics systems.

That is the conclusion of a new report from the non-profit RAND Corporation, which has been working with the military for several years to streamline its logistics systems. The report also found improvements in military air distribution for operations in Bosnia and Kuwait.

While the report was just issued this spring, it does not examine logistical support for operations in Iraq. A separate report on that subject is in final stages of preparation and is expected out later this year (see sidebar page 33).

According to Marc Robbins, a RAND senior policy analyst and an author of the new report, key factors contributing to the system improvements included:

- Greater transparency of information, with "systems feedback end to end, so we could see where the problems are."

A C-17 takes off from Afghanistan after delivering supplies.

- Improved cooperation between providers of transportation and their customers. Robbins notes that previously, TRANSCOM (the U.S. Transportation Command) "had a reputation for not always trying to figure out what kind of service customers needed. This time around there was a much stronger desire to sit down with the customers."

- Overcoming some bureaucratic obstacles for the kind of service needed.

All of this is based on lean principles.

"The basic idea of lean is don't let anything stop moving," Robbins notes. "Keep the minimum on hand, throughput and flow are always better than work in process. Don't let local optimizations get in the way of overall optimization. We learned we cannot worry so much about building the perfect pallet or filling up a plane. You just have to keep it moving."

Years in the Works

RAND has been working with the military to improve logistics

The Report on Iraq

RAND Corporation is finalizing a study of logistics in support of U.S. military operations in Iraq. Draft recommendations are going to Army leaders, and a final report should be issued in several months, according to RAND analyst Marc Robbins.

Recent news reports have described problems with logistics in Iraq. For example, in February 2004, The New York Times reported that an unclassified study of Iraq operations found a "morass" of supply shortages, including tank engines sitting on warehouse shelves with no drivers to transport them, artillery units cannibalizing captured Iraqi guns to keep their own howitzers working, and Army medics foraging supplies from combat hospitals. The Times story said that, according to the report, the Third Infantry Division was within two weeks of being halted by a lack of spare parts.

Robbins declined to discuss the new RAND report until it is officially released. However, he did comment that in Iraq, "the operational tempo is far, far higher. It creates a huge demand on the supply system."

since the late 1990s. Several efforts were launched, achieving gains, within the individual services, such as the Army's Velocity Management initiative (*Lean Manufacturing Advisor*, September 2002), the Air Force's Lean Logistics and the Marine Corps' Precision Logistics.

These all grew out of the fact that logistics support through the 1990s was, according to the new report, "often poor and unreliable, and customers were losing confidence in it."

The report also notes that during the first Persian Gulf war in 1990, there were "significant" problems with logistics support; "distribution times were long, variable, and undependable, due largely to inefficient processes, clogged ports and a myriad of other problems."

In early 2000, leaders of TRANSCOM and the Defense Logistics Agency (DLA), launched the Strategic Distribution program (SD), an improvement initiative encompassing all branches of the military.

The earlier initiatives did achieve benefits. In fact, Robbins says, the practices of the Army's Velocity Management effort, which focused on deliveries to permanent installations, "has become embedded in the Army," although it is now called Army Distribution Management. "We have permanent teams that go and work with units that are supported out of the Army."

But a broader effort was needed to achieve the greatest gains needed to support a multi-branch deployment (as is now the case in Iraq).

Strategic Distribution is built around what are known as the "3 S's": stock positioning, scheduled movements and synchronization.

Stock positioning means putting inventory in the right place, primarily at two strategic distribution sites, one on each coast.

Scheduled movements are, in effect, milk runs; trucks leave the strategic sites at a certain time each day and arrive at their destination at a set time.

And these steps are **synchronized** to minimize queuing and holding times.

This approach is producing savings that RAND projects will be $120 million over the five years from 2003 to 2007. The savings are from consolidating distribution facilities and less use of services such as FedEx, for example.

End-to-End Service

But the real test of SD came with Operation Enduring Freedom (OEF), the military operation in Afghanistan.

Since there was nothing exactly like that operation to which logistics performance could be compared, RAND looked at how well troops were supplied during operations in Bosnia and Kuwait from January 1997 until August 2001. RAND also spoke extensively with military personnel about their experience in receiving supplies.

In both cases, after the SD initiative was launched in 2000, the monthly average number of days for end-to-end distribution time dropped, and variability in the process also declined.

Supplies for troops in Afghanistan were delivered to a staging point in Uzbekistan. RAND found that the average end-to-end delivery time to that location during OEF was 16 days — shorter than delivery times for Kosovo, Bosnia and Kuwait before SD was implemented. However, during the same time period (the last quarter of 2001), which was after SD had been launched, the end-to-end times had dropped to 12 days for Kosovo, 9 days for Bosnia and 8 days for Kuwait.

In making the comparisons, RAND notes that shipments to Ukbekistan involved much greater distance from U.S. distribution points and a greater number of cargo "touches" than any of the other locations.

In Kuwait, September 1999, military leaders were so dissatisfied with logistics support that they contracted with a commercial air carrier to supply the troops. Service was switched back to the military in April 2001 (after SD was in place), on the understanding that service and price would have to match those of the commercial firm. They did.

The Kuwait experience aside, the military has generally avoided using commercial planes; now they use whatever is available. "This was a major advance for them," Robbins states. "The standard was preference for organic aircraft. Usually what they would do is let cargo build up. It was a sustained problem, and only when it becomes clear the problem is not going to go away" would commercial aircraft be hired.

That changed after the Sept. 11 terrorist attacks, when most military aircraft were deployed and not available for logistics support. Private carriers were used more extensively; the fact that commercial air traffic dropped significantly after the attacks meant significant capacity was available.

A Better System

Other strategies, technologies and techniques have contributed to improvements in military logistics operations. One is extensive use of the Internet and radio frequency identification (RFID) technology.

"In general, the improvements in transparency and communication up and down the chain are much better now," says Robbins. "The Internet makes it much easier to move information around. It's nice to be able to actually see things as they move through the system. It's even better to have this wide-ranging network so we can move data around to people who actually need it."

Another positive move is that last fall Defense Secretary Donald Rumsfeld officially designated TRANSCOM the DPO, or distribution process owner. While TRANSCOM does not actually "own" all aspects of the distribution process, the agency is responsible for overseeing the end-to-end process, assisting in activity and putting pressure on other agencies when necessary.

A related move is the creation of DDOCs, or deployment distribution operations centers. The first of these is a 70-person operation set up in Kuwait to help manage support of the troops there.

Asked about the state of military logistics today, Robbins comments, "I think we're far ahead of where we were in Desert Storm. We have much greater visibility and reliability, a much better feedback loop. It's not perfect, there are lots of breakdowns, but it's a far better system. We're getting much closer to supporting an expeditionary force."

TAKEAWAYS

- Lean principles help troops receive better support.
- All parties to the supply chain must cooperate.
- Information should be readily available everywhere.

Part II
Building Partnerships

OVERVIEW

A supply chain transformation can only take place when you have strong working relationships based on trust with your suppliers and customers. How you build trust and establish relationships is the topic of the chapters in this section.

Several manufacturers, including JDS Uniphase, Pratt & Whitney and Visteon, as well as some suppliers, spoke at a conference about the importance of understanding each other and carefully planning joint lean efforts. Their comments are described in Chapter Six.

Understanding can be established through a four-step approach to the supply chain. That, at least, was the approach of Lockheed Martin, which is outlined in Chapter Seven. The essential elements of the four steps can be utilized by any company.

It also helps to understand the extent to which your suppliers have already become lean. Chapter Eight explains how John Deere developed a metric, called Manufacturing Critical-path Time, to help them assess a supplier's agility and the risk involved in using any particular supplier.

Another well-defined, carefully planned approach is described in Chapter Nine. The approach, developed by Northrop Grumman, was the basis for a program of helping suppliers become lean, and enabled the company to target the suppliers most suited to the program.

dj Orthopedics wanted to reduce its number of suppliers and streamline its supply chain. The company understood that achieving a better understanding of its suppliers was the key to achieving those goals, a story told in Chapter 10.

Chapter 11 focuses on a different type of company – motorcycle manufacturer Harley Davidson. Learn how Harley, faced with a need to expand capacity, worked with its suppliers to help them gain capacity as well, but without buying new equipment.

Not all efforts to work with suppliers go smoothly. Chapter 12 tells the story of how it took Rockwell Collins several years of working with one of its suppliers to find the approach that finally benefited both companies.

Working with customers can be just as important as working with suppliers. Xerox, a company profiled in Chapter 13, not only helps its customers, but has made lean and six sigma part of the customer services it offers, seeing its approach as a way to gain a competitive advantage.

And Chapter 14 tells the tale of Trek Bicycle, which benefits itself by helping bicycle dealers improve their repair operations, creating additional capacity for selling the bicycles Trek manufactures.

6

Customers—and Suppliers— Offer Tips for Working With Suppliers

June, 2001

Managers pursuing lean transformations in a variety of production environments exchanged ideas about how they are working with suppliers at the 5th Annual Supply Chain Management Forum sponsored by Productivity, Inc.

Kathleen Strevel, director of operations for the electro-optical division of JDS Uniphase in Bloomfield, Conn., said the maker of fiber optic modulators wanted to have some lean successes before recommending that suppliers make the journey. Her unit has been pursuing lean since 1997 as a way to cope with strong growth driven by the burgeoning use of the internet.

"We're probably far enough along so that change has become the norm," she said about the lean effort. "We expect it. We're at that stage now where momentum is growing.

She said the unit followed a "cook book" approach to lean, beginning with product-focused cells and visual controls and progressing toward continuous flow. One of the current priorities is to better balance the work elements within cells, many of which have small ovens for curing processes. The unit is organized into product-focused cell layout of the plant allows cells to be configured for a product or reconfigured rapidly for a different product so output can flex with demand.

Strevel estimated that about 20 percent of the unit's components are purchased and 80 percent are made in-house. That was in sharp contrast to attendees from older industrial companies with traditional supply chains delivering as much as 80 percent of components.

Telecom Travails

Despite the relatively small ratio of parts purchased by the JDS unit, company officials noted that suppliers of components and capital equipment were critically important due to the telecommunication market's fast technological change and supply chain immaturity.

"Everything is new and leading edge. We're working with a lot of mom-and-pop shops with twelve people working for them," said Supply Line Manager Kristen Wells. Additionally, she said telecomm companies must plan for price reductions of 15 to 20 percent annually and product life cycles of five years or less.

She said suppliers fall into four categories, which affects how JDS manages the relationship:

1. Sole supplier: There is only one company providing the product, so you must try to establish solid relationships with long-term agreements. "The better the relationship, the better you can weather the peaks and valleys" of the telecom market.

2. Technical/complex: There is a strong reliance on the supplier for design and process development. "The engineers will be talking to one another" in this relationship as well as the managers.

3. Integrated: The supplier makes your design with a qualified process. These qualified suppliers earn a share of the business.

4. Commodity: You can get the material anytime and any-where. The use of auctions and competitive bidding are fac-tors in these relationships.

The JDS supply line management philosophy stresses treating sup-pliers with respect, integrity, and fairness. That means holding them accountable for performance and quality, avoiding one-sided agreements, sharing forecasts and technical information, avoiding an attack on supplier margin and bringing them along on the lean journey. "We were realizing that we really couldn't improve our cycle times and lead times until we got to the supply base," said Wells.

The internal lean efforts at JDS meant it could react to the mar-ket's ups and downs by adjusting takt times, but suppliers could only do so with inventory, said Michael O'Connor, a JDS contin-uous improvement manager who helps suppliers implement lean. The goal of the lean effort is to help key suppliers eliminate waste so JDS can meet demand and price pressures and the suppliers can maintain margins. "We want them here in the future," he said.

Educating Management

Criteria for identifying the vital few suppliers includes, among other factors, spending history, quality problems, and those that support multiple JDS units. The company prefers to bring suppli-er company managers to JDS to view the lean changes and partic-ipate in kaizen events, explained O'Connor.

Suppliers actually see what lean is and "get a flavor for what an event is," he said. That's important because "we have a very young supply base." A key supplier could be a company consisting of "a PhD and six guys with master's degrees" who just created a new fiber optic device. Typically, they have little experience with mass production and even less with lean.

Work with suppliers begins by trying to secure the commitment of senior management. If executives agree to support the lean con-version, they attend a continuous improvement workshop for management that is run by JDS, said O'Connor. The workshop gives executives an introduction to lean concepts and the tools. The benefits for suppliers of participating include:

- Getting more business

- Higher quality, shorter lead time

- Increased capacity

- Cost savings

Management's education continues with a visit to a JDS plant where lean production is being used. Executives also are expected to participate in a kaizen event. JDS provides the training; suppliers pick up hotel and meal costs.

Members of the continuous improvement office from JDS then map the supplier's current state and determine what production lines are good candidates for cellular production. An improvement plan is developed that shows "where we want to concentrate our efforts," said O'Connor.

People from the JDS continuous improvement office facilitate kaizen events at supplier facilities. Supplier performance is judged on the technology, quality, responsiveness, delivery and cost.

Hearing from Suppliers

Two suppliers told attendees about their JDS-guided efforts at lean. Jim Bray, plant manager of an AFL Photonics plant in Norton, Mass., said the lean effort began in late 2000 with education aimed at all levels, including senior managers. Process flows that looked "like somebody had thrown a plate of spaghetti at a chart" when mapped, have been converted to product-focused cells. Cells contain only the equipment and material needed to satisfy daily demand, he said. JDS gives the plant a monthly forecast and a daily fax of what is needed. Results have included:

- 80 percent reduction in work-in-process (WIP)

- 40 percent space reduction

- 27 percent travel distance reduction

- 50 percent lead time reduction

- 29 percent productivity increase

During a tour of the JDS plant, attendees got a chance to see and hear from the second supplier. Leo LeBoeuf, operations manager for RIFOCS Corporation, said his company moved a process from a California facility to a cell inside the JDS Connecticut plant in 2000. Previously, modulators were shipped from Connecticut to California to have connectors installed, the last step in the product's value stream. The coast-to-coast air shipments created expense, a one- to two-week lead time, and risked damage to delicate optical fibers.

"There had to be a better way, and the better way was a lean manufacturing cell," said LeBoeuf. Modulators from a JDS cell nearby are brought over to the RIFOCS cell in small batches. LeBoeuf said JDS tells him a week in advance the "range" of parts it anticipates needing on a daily basis for the next week. There are no purchase orders, except for special jobs. RIFOCS owns the equipment in the cell, and pays the employees. JDS gets special pricing on the parts for taking out RIFOCS overhead by providing the space in its plant.

"If this were an adversarial relationship, this wouldn't work," he noted. A customer must be "results oriented" and willing to communicate for such an in-house relationship to work, he said.

RIFOCS is alerted to change orders through a link to the JDS computer system. At the cell's first station, an operator wands a bar code on the modulator package. The JDS system recognizes if a change order has been issued and sends the information to the computer screen at the station.

Aerospace Goals

Jet engine maker Pratt & Whitney's supply chain is the opposite of JDSs environment. It purchases 80 percent of its components and makes 20 percent. "So unless we are able to work with our suppliers and make them better we're not going to be successful," said Bob Francis, manager, continuous improvement. Francis provides training and guidance about lean to the company's international suppliers. "I have to come in and sell" suppliers on going lean.

It's an important sales job. The company needs a supply chain committed to improvement to meet its own stretch goals of:

- Reducing quality escapes by 30 percent

- Cutting lead times to less than 20 weeks, as measured from order to ship

- Achieving 96 percent on-time delivery

- Cutting costs by 30 percent year over year

Francis uses these same measures when identifying which suppliers are most in need of help. They also help to move the customer-supplier relationship beyond a focus on margins. "Do you really care what the supplier's margin is?" he asked.

The process of working with a supplier begins with an assessment of the supplier's plant, based on the principles of the Toyota Production System. Next, Pratt works with the supplier to develop a continuous improvement plan based on the assessment results. Development of the plan covers:

Organization

- Build management awareness of lean through training.

- Identify a continuous improvement manager and what senior manager he or she will report to.

Training

- Teach the basic lean tools of 5S, standard work, total productive maintenance (TPM), set-up reduction, and quality improvement.

Business goals

- Identify no more than 10 metrics that will measure improvement, such as lead time reduction, quality escape reduction, cost reduction, and defect reduction.

Identify continuous improvement target areas

- Create a performance chart showing the gap between the current status and the goals.

- List equipment, products.

- Divide products into families.

- Determine where production cells and supermarkets can be created.

Improvement Projects

- Create a list of improvement projects for the next 6 to 12 months by department or cell, the type of improvement to be done, product or part name affected by the project, when it will be done, and the expected results. Long-term agreements with suppliers stipulate how many kaizen events they must run along with shared cost savings or price reductions.

- Develop a kaizen promotion office staffed by at least one full-time member who can manage the improvement activity and influence others. This person should have middle management experience enthusiasm, and have been a leader on at least two kaizen teams.

This is followed by two continuous improvement or kaizen workshops on the shop floor followed by a train-the-trainer course for the members of the supplier team that will spread the lean conversion. A third kaizen workshop follows. At this point, "the training wheels come off," said Francis, and the supplier is responsible for rolling out the continuous improvement plan.

Automotive

Thomas Rogge and Graeme Edgson, lean manufacturing managers at Visteon, said earlier internal lean improvement efforts at the giant parts maker failed because they focused on improving the performance of individual processes, rather than the whole system.

In reaction, the company developed the Visteon Production System to take a value stream approach that could be extended to suppliers and customers. Not surprisingly, mapping value streams is a key improvement activity.

The company is migrating toward electronic pull signals with suppliers, but they recommended beginning with a kanban card system to give people the knowledge and discipline needed to operate pull systems successfully. Visteon is piloting an electronic pull system at a plant and its suppliers, they noted. The system allows suppliers to view a real time part usage report through the web. Ultimately, the system will allow production operators to pull parts directly to line side based on actual consumption and to extend that information out to suppliers.

TAKEAWAYS

- Different types of suppliers require different supply chain strategies.
- The volume of business with a supplier does not necessarily determine how critical that supplier is.
- Strategy should be thoroughly planned in advance.

7

4 Steps for Deploying Lean "Blueprint" Through the Supply Chain

April, 2000

Your organization is committed to implementing lean and TPM, but how do you get your supply chain to fly in formation?

Consider the carrot-and-stick approach adopted by Lockheed Martin Aeronautics Company. It requires suppliers to cut costs, cycle times, and prices (stick), but gives them advice and hands-on help with kaizen events to get them started (carrot).

Lockheed Martin launched the lean supply chain effort in early 1999 with two pilot suppliers. The process was further refined and presented at a supplier conference in September 1999. The company told the 250 attending suppliers that they had to implement lean if they wanted to remain suppliers. Each vendor had to submit a lean conversion plan. By mid-February, 213 had.

Lockheed Martin now is refining the plans with suppliers and helping others begin implementation. "We have a very good supply chain," said Mike Walters, vice president, Aeronautics Company Materials Management. "We'd like to go and help them all, but we don't have the resources ourselves to do our total supply base."

Protecting Profit Levels

Lockheed Martin began attacking costs, quality, and cycle times when it launched an internal lean effort in the first quarter of 1998. The effort is aimed at winning new business in the turbulence of today's competitive aerospace market. The old business model of adding profit to expected costs to arrive at the price of government contracts just doesn't fly any longer. Lockheed Martin is telling suppliers, they "can't live in that model anymore," said Walters.

Lean offers Lockheed Martin and suppliers a way to maintain profit levels by cutting costs and cycle times so they can win business by offering customers affordable aircraft. "We just can't afford to pay suppliers as much total money as we used to," said Walters. "None of our customers has as much money as it used to." With suppliers representing 50-to-60 percent of product costs, "we know we can't win new business without their help," he said.

Walters and Terry Hoppe, a Material Management lean facilitator, talked to us about the process being used to create a lean supply chain:

1. Identify and prioritize suppliers to work with and gather information to establish cost and cycle time reduction targets.

As a first step, Material Management and production representatives at three main manufacturing locations selected the suppliers to work with, based on such factors as costs and the critical nature of their products. The company selected production suppliers for the F-22, F-16, C-130J and critical suppliers for the Joint Strike Fighter programs.

Next, Material Management *made sure a supplier's management understood the objectives of the lean conversion and would support the process.* "Most of the things you do in lean are free except for the manpower that it takes," observed Walters. Suppliers had to commit to making people available for lean projects.

Suppliers had to agree to reduction targets in cycle times, costs, and defects. They also signed memorandums of agreement (MOA) with Lockheed Martin specifying price reductions on current and future purchase orders. "We're not after their margins, we're just after costs," explained Walters.

2. Engagement and team formation.

During the engagement process, lean facilitators from Material Management met with the suppliers to review lean targets. "We tell them at that time we want to execute the MOA, which will give tangible results in cost, cycle time, and quality," Walters said.

In addition, the suppliers must form kaizen teams and designate a lean "champion," who will be responsible for the supplier's lean effort. This sends a clear message that Lockheed Martin "can't do it for you," said Walters. "Only you can do it. You have to make people available. We're here to help facilitate."

Kaizen teams are cross-functional and cross-company for Lockheed Martin and each supplier. There are no permanent teams. They are selected based on the nature of the kaizen events. For instance, people from different functions are needed for improving product flow compared to administrative areas.

Material Management facilitates a baseline assessment and three subsequent kaizen events at the supplier, who must commit to dates for the events. The champion at each supplier has the authority to approve process changes recommended by the kaizen teams. "They are, in effect, the change agents," said Walters.

3. Baseline assessment and continuous improvement plan.

Hoppe described the five-day baseline assessment as capturing the "as-is" condition of the supplier's facility. "We select product families on the critical path and map the whole value stream inside the supplier's four walls from shipping to receiving," he said. Lockheed Martin facilitators look at three value streams:

1. Product flow – This covers the physical flow of parts between suppliers and Lockheed and what it does with parts when they arrive.

Source: Lockheed Martin Material Management

Workstation Improvements – Lockheed Martin's lean supply chain effort dramatically improved an electronic assembly area at a supplier during a recent kaizen event. The "before" picture, left, shows clutter and several kits being worked on, causing quality and tracking problems. After improvement, the clutter is gone. A system of kanban squares taped to the workstation surface limits the number of kits being worked on to one by visually signaling a material handler to bring a new kit only when it is needed. Other improvements included:

	Before	After	Improvement
Machine Setup Time	2-4 hours	0.5 –1 hour	-75%
Operator Setup Time	20 minutes	1-2 minutes	-92%
Tool Quantity	150	20	-87%
Process Documentation	50 pages	1 page	-98%

2. Information flow – This includes how Lockheed Martin gives suppliers schedule data and how it receives cost data back. "We must find ways to share cost data back and forth faster, and we have to find a way to get proposals in a week instead of 60 days," said Walters. The ultimate goal is to cut cycle times so Lockheed Martin and suppliers can deliver an airplane to customer demand, rather than a set lead time.

3. Technical problem solving – This stream includes engineering changes and quality improvements. This value stream is more likely than the other two to require capital investments or customer approvals related to changes to the product.

Supplier personnel participate in the mapping exercises as team members and leaders, walking the value streams with paper and pencil to collect information and map the processes.

Before the mapping begins at a facility, Lockheed Martin facilitators make sure kaizen team members will have face-to-face access to people who might have key information about processes. "If we walk up to a machine operator, they know why we are there in advance," Hoppe said. This is crucial to the collection of first-hand information about process steps.

The assessment also creates a "future state map" showing how the values streams should look, if they were lean. "*Going from current state to future becomes our blueprint [for continuous improvement],*" said Hoppe.

Lockheed Martin is discovering that suppliers add value about one to five percent of the time with their current manufacturing processes. That's right in line with industry in general.

Even among suppliers claiming to be lean, Lockheed Martin finds that the typical value stream adds value to material only 5 percent of the time. The other 95 percent consists of nonvalue-adding activities such as storage, rework, transportation, etc.

Lockheed Martin wants to boost the ratio of value-adding to non-value-adding time to 50/50 in manufacturing and 80/20 in assembly. "They represent world-class status and are extremely challenging goals to hit," said Hoppe.

4. Continuous improvement events.

Implementing the lean blueprint usually begins with a radical change (kaikaku) event followed by two continuous improvement (kaizen) events. The events last five days, combining classroom work and shop-floor activities aimed at eliminating the nonvalue-adding activities identified by the value stream maps.

"We're basically there for the baseline and three follow-on events," explained Hoppe. Suppliers are responsible for continuing the progress towards a lean future state.

Lockheed Martin and suppliers establish a timetable and goals for the first three improvement events. "This is not a science project," said Walters. "This is about continuous improvement. It's about getting results and it's about celebrating the success of those results."

The champions at the supplier companies are responsible for implementing the lean conversion plan. Material Management reviews progress weekly.

So far, kaikaku or kaizen events have been done with 18 major suppliers. Another 20 major suppliers and 50 smaller suppliers will host events in 2000.

After Lockheed Martin facilitates the baseline assessment and the first three improvement events, the supplier who has received the assistance still has a strong incentive to continue the lean effort. Suppliers had to describe how they were going to sustain lean activities in the conversion plans submitted after the September 1999 conference. And they have price targets to meet in the MOA.

"The expectation is we will set a reduction target to be achieved over the life" of existing contracts with suppliers, explained Walters. And when Lockheed Martin is ready to make the next round of purchases from suppliers, it expects to see improvements in costs, cycle times, and quality reflected in the price.

TAKEAWAYS

- Suppliers should be evaluated and ranked to identify those with whom you work to reduce cost and cycle time.
- The right team must be established to work with suppliers.
- Assessments, improvement plans and improvement events must be ongoing.

8

A New Metric Measures Suppliers

July, 2005

John Deere couldn't find a way to measure the "leanness" of its suppliers, so the company created one, developing a new metric. Combined with efforts to help suppliers become more lean, the metric has helped shorten lead times, increase flexibility and reduce Deere's risk of lost sales.

In addition, the approach has improved the company's ability to decide which parts can be obtained from overseas and which should not.

John Deere calls its metric Manufacturing Critical-Path Time, or MCT. It is defined as the typical amount of calendar time from when a manufacturing order is created through the critical path until the first, single piece of that order is delivered to the customer.

The idea, according to Paul Ericksen, enterprise supplier development lead for worldwide supply chain management at John Deere, is to "identify the critical path of the supplier's manufacturing and logistics to get the parts to our user factory." Calculation of MCT assumes the supplier has all the raw material needed to make John Deere's order on hand, and it assumes the supplier has no work in process or finished goods inventory in the pipeline.

What does this tell Deere? "Say the supplier is used to producing to forecast," Ericksen explains. "If you make a significant rise in what the forecast is, MCT tells you how fast you can react to that significant rise."

Moreover, Deere uses the metric to help evaluate supplier bids. A decision to award a bid will not be based on price alone. For example, on a particular part, an overseas supplier might offer a lower price than a domestic supplier. However, if the overseas company has a much longer MCT than the domestic company, Deere will add a penalty of a certain percentage to the bid.

"MCT is a tremendous indicator of the amount of risk you are assuming," Ericksen states. "If you are working with a supplier with an MCT of 13 weeks vs. 1 week, you have a higher risk with the 13-week supplier of them causing you to lose sales."

Calculating that risk and determining what penalty to assign for a longer MCT is challenging. "Whenever you are trying to assign a cost to risk, some of it is art, some of it is science, some of it is just talking to all the old guys who have had to deal with it over the years. Then there is the red-face test: Does this make sense? We look at the times we actually did lose sales."

The process does not mean domestic suppliers are always chosen ahead of overseas suppliers. "It makes us make more intelligent choices," says Ericksen. "If you are ordering from a supplier, and it's a very mature product that rarely changes in design, and you don't have to account for the ability to supply additional product to market, the risk of losing sales is less than if you have a forecast that isn't very accurate, and you have to have the ability to produce more than is in the forecast in a short term."

Ericksen adds, "This is not anti-overseas sourcing. It's another way of getting at the true, accurate total acquisition cost. I've seen a lot of companies go out and source the wrong things overseas."

A Need for Speed

John Deere is part of Moline, Ill.-based Deere & Co., which reported sales of $10.7 billion for the six months ending April 30, 2005 (up 13 percent) and net income of $826.8 million for the period, up from $648.1 million for the same period in 2004. Deere's products include agricultural, forestry and power equipment.

The John Deere unit makes lawn mowers — which is what drove the effort leading to the development of MCT.

Seventy percent of the company's lawn mowers are sold in the spring, during a period of less than four months. When the company first got into the lawn mower business, "we looked at our entire order fulfillment process. What we found out is that it was probably modeled more for delivering tractors and combines to farmers than to delivering to consumers," Ericksen notes.

"How do we get the supply chain leaned out so that it would be agile enough to react to market trends? We can't have months of lead time to react to those trends. We knew we needed to address the supply chain flexibility."

Internally, John Deere is fairly lean. "Typically, we can produce lawn mowers in minutes or hours, once we have the raw material," he explains. "Where's the benefit for us in further tweaking our internal processes? We're always doing that, but the big bang for the buck is to work with the parts of your extended enterprise, your suppliers, who haven't done this yet."

Getting information from suppliers to calculate their MCTs has not been difficult, Ericksen says: "It's a very non-threatening metric. Typically, when OEM customers go into their suppliers and focus on waste, they're focusing on cost. The supplier translates that into 'you need a lower price from us.' They're very reluctant on sharing costs. But when you ask what their MCT is, it's not as threatening. It's easier to put together, and it's something a customer should be able to ask a supplier for."

The result of John Deere's efforts, according to Ericksen, is that the supply base was set up, the company won business from Home Depot in 2002, and "we were able to execute almost flawlessly." More recently, John Deere won business from Lowe's. "If we didn't know the flexibility of our supply chain, or the inflexibility, and didn't set up contingencies to plan for the inflexibility, we couldn't support our customers," he declares.

Moreover, given the short selling period, if John Deere can't deliver product because a supplier doesn't deliver parts or materials, there is no time to make up the lost sales. "When customers are looking for John Deere mowers in the spring, and the grass is growing, and we don't have them, they're going to go to a competitor," notes Ericksen.

Furthering Improvement

John Deere doesn't just apply a metric to its suppliers; it helps them become lean. Executives work with suppliers to develop current and future state value stream maps and process maps, to identify areas ripe for improvement.

"Sometimes they can address it on their own, sometimes they need our help," says Ericksen. John Deere may connect the supplier with a unit of the Manufacturing Extension Partnership, a nationwide network of government-funded consultants who work with small and mid-sized companies to help them improve, often through implementation of lean techniques.

"Once we've set up a baseline that says there is a lean gap, it doesn't matter whose lean program they use to close the gap as long as it is closed," he adds.

Ericksen observes, "I think there is a misperception out there that most manufacturing in the U.S. is lean. A lot of our suppliers don't have big engineering departments. They focus on getting new business, then on getting product out the door every day. A significant portion of the suppliers out there aren't lean."

Focusing on MCT yields a range of benefits, Ericksen states, commenting, "We have seen that when a supplier becomes leaner, their quality, delivery and cost all improve."

MCT is also spreading throughout Deere & Co.

"Business needs drove how this metric has evolved," he explains. "It started out in lawn and grounds care. We had a different customer. We really had to focus on lean order fulfillment. We introduced it and proved the metric out. Now we're adopted it across the entire enterprise for a couple of years — agriculture, construction, power systems — but the business need drove us to do this first."

TAKEAWAYS

- Knowing how agile a supplier is can help you evaluate that supplier.
- Making your extended enterprise lean significantly increases your own agility.
- Suppliers may be very accepting of efforts to decrease their lead time.

9

Lean Supply Chain Effort Is Built On Research, Planning & Structure

June, 2005

If you want to work with your suppliers to make your supply chain lean, do your homework.

Northrop Grumman did. Executives at the company's shipbuilding facility in Newport News, Va., began a program with suppliers in 2003. They carefully targeted which suppliers they wanted in the program, developed detailed plans setting goals and expectations, and contracted with a nationwide network of consultants to make the initiative work.

"You really need to make sure that you've done your due diligence in terms of looking at suppliers who are going to make a difference," says John Jordan, director of sourcing at the facility. "You can't just randomly pick them. You need to make a conscious stratification of your supply base."

The effort has already achieved notable benefits. The first group of suppliers involved (there have been four groups so far) achieved improvements in:

- Lead time, with gains averaging 35 percent.

- On-time delivery, 44 percent.

Efforts by Northrop Grumman's Dock to Stock Value Stream Team improved operational flow and led to consolidation of personnel from two buildings into one. One area transformed is shown in its before (top) and after states.

- Inventory turns, 35 percent.

- First-pass acceptance rate, 62 percent.

Further, the effort is helping Northrop Grumman turn at least some supplier relationships into partnerships, leading to long-term supply agreements that Jordan says are resulting in "multi-million dollar savings," though he declined to provide specific figures.

A Need for Speed

The sprawling Newport News facility builds and overhauls aircraft carriers and submarines for the U.S. Navy. Occupying 550 acres along two miles of waterfront, the facility includes numerous buildings, seven dry docks with one floating dry dock, four piers and the largest gantry crane in the western hemisphere. Not quite half of all spending relates to new construction of carriers, with the remainder divided almost evenly between submarine construction and overhauls.

Northrop Grumman is under pressure from the Navy to do all work as quickly as possible, and "we simply don't have a significant amount of lead time in many cases to get material delivered," Jordan notes. "We need components, and we need them in many cases in days or weeks as opposed to months." A ship may come in for overhaul, for example, and workers may discover it needs a new valve, which may be a specialized part with complex engineering. "It's not like you can go to Wal-Mart or Lowe's or Home Depot and just get a valve," he quips.

Targeting Suppliers

The Newport News sector has been on a lean journey since 1996, though by its own admission, the effort was fragmented until about 2002 when an overall enterprise approach was established. That effort provided the basis for supply chain improvements; "We felt we shouldn't be asking suppliers to do something we were not doing ourselves," says Jordan.

A Supplier Sees a Win-Win Partnership

Revcar Fasteners is happy to be giving Northrop Grumman a better price on its products than in the past because the company is getting more business from its customer. And that is a direct result of Revcar's participation in Northrop Grumman's lean supply chain program, which is leading to a stronger partnership between the two companies.

"This really is a partnership," says Jamie Farrell, sales manager with Revcar. "Northrop Grumman is taking the time and money to train us and make us understand their industry better. Typically, we go in and show a customer how we can save them money, but we don't always learn how their business works."

Since 2003, Revcar has been getting an education about Northrop Grumman's Newport News shipyard. The two companies have done business together for years, but the new partnership is leading to a deeper understanding of processes at the shipyard, resulting in Revcar providing better service.

Revcar is a distributor of fasteners to OEMs. A division of the Wurth Group, Revcar has about 100 employees and sales of around $30 million. According to Farrell, sales to Northrop Grumman are "in the millions."

The distributor was part of the second group of suppliers invited by Northrop Grumman to be part of its lean supply chain efforts — and Farrell admits that, initially, her company was skeptical.

"Number one, the concern was 'how much is this going to cost us?'" she recalls. "The second concern was 'how much time is it going to take? How many man-hours is it going to take for our employees to implement these lean procedures?"

However, the initial presentation by Northrop Grumman was persuasive, and Revcar climbed on board. The first significant change was establishment of a vendor-managed inventory (VMI) program at Newport News, with Revcar in charge of a new supermarket of parts at the facility.

Farrell explains: "They had a warehouse with racks that go up 20

In launching what the company calls lean supply chain management, executives knew it simply was not feasible to involve every one of the sector's 2,600 suppliers. (That number, by the way, is

feet in the air. The fasteners were spread out. They would get a requisition, and come into the warehouse for one part. They would drive a forklift, and bring the pallet down, count out 100 pieces, then bag it up. It would then be sent out into the yard somewhere. To pull a part could take half an hour. Now, with VMI, we have 400 part numbers all in a central location. It's a two-bin kanban program. A warehouse employee will walk over to the area and count out what they need. A Revcar Fastener employee comes in three times a week. Everything is bar-coded. They scan the empty bins and replenish them."

More recently, Revcar and Northrop Grumman have been creating value stream maps of facility operations, showing the flow of parts from the warehouse. That effort has made it clear, Farrell says, that "what we need to do is take it to the next level. We need to take some of these 400 parts and put them in the shop, what we call the point of use."

Farrell believes that one of the biggest benefits of the new effort is the partnership between the two companies.

"Now we're sharing information," she says. "We are finding out what parts are critical. We have a better understanding of how the shipyard works and why delivery is crucial, why we need to have a quote into them on time. By working as a partnership, we're finding out they are going to use X amount of this part. We know what their demand for this fastener is going to be throughout the year, or two years or three years. We know we're going to sell this part to them for the next three years. We look at it as a win-win because we can buy it cheaper. And they do save money. If they say 'quote this part, and we're going to work with you as a partnership, and you will supply this partnership for the next three years,' they get a better price."

In addition, Revcar's increased understanding of lean principles is helping the distributor with its other customers. "I can talk intelligently now to a global sourcing manager who is working with these same principles," Farrell states. "That's critical in our business, to bring new ideas to the table. We are definitely a service-oriented company selling what most people consider a commodity."

down significantly from what it had been in the year 2000 because of a conscious effort to "right-size" the supply base.)

So the company targeted suppliers providing pipes, valves and fit-

tings, which Jordan says are among the biggest cost-drivers overall
— "several thousand mechanics are dependent on those particular
commodities," he explains.

Valerie Smith, manager of supplier quality, played a critical role in
the selection and implementation processes.

Fifty-one suppliers are actively involved in lean initiatives so far —
only a fraction of the total number of suppliers, but those 51 represent almost 40 percent of the company's receipt volume, according to Jordan.

Northrop Grumman's goals for the program are reductions in
price premiums, expediting and inventory levels, as well as
improved material availability. For suppliers, the expected benefits
include reductions in cycle time and inventory levels, increased
capacity, and improvements in agility and profitability. Together,
the two sides hope to achieve stronger partnerships, improved
communication, an agile supply chain, improved profitability and
strong performance on contracts.

Letter of Commitment

The first challenge in launching the supplier program was getting
suppliers to take part. Jordan says he was surprised to learn, when
the first group of selected suppliers was approached, that simply
inviting them to take part wasn't enough. With subsequent groups
(there are a total of four groups so far), top managers from each
supplier were invited to take part in a one-day, hands-on introduction to lean concepts and principles — a tactic that led to many
more suppliers agreeing to take part.

Northrop Grumman set up the effort in partnership with the
Manufacturing Extension Partnership, a nationwide network of
non-profit, government funded organizations that help small and
mid-sized business to become more efficient, largely through
application of lean principles.

The Virginia Philpott MEP, the local organization, became the lead consultant and training organization. However, MEPs in a variety of other states, from Massachusetts to Oregon, are also involved, working with suppliers in those locations.

Each supplier that signs up for the program signs a letter of understanding making certain commitments. The first is that the supplier undergoes a lean assessment by MEP officials, which is paid for by Northrop Grumman. (The cost is roughly $2,500 per supplier.) This determines the state of the supplier's lean knowledge and capabilities, and includes general recommendations for improvement activities.

(Jordan characterizes most suppliers as being in the beginning stages of a lean journey.)

Subsequently, the supplier and Northrop Grumman split evenly the cost of consulting work to implement those improvements, up to a total cost of $50,000. (The typical cost is around $35,000.) That amount is strictly for the consulting; it does not include any capital spending that may be required of the supplier to achieve additional improvements.

Keeping Score

A chief focus of the efforts is to improve the supplier's agility — which is defined as "a supplier's ability to provide for and reliably react to short notice changes in quantities and quick delivery with minimum inventory levels." Elements contributing to agility are lead time, on-time delivery, inventory turns and quality.

According to Northrop Grumman, agility gains by the first group of suppliers include:

- More than $3.9 million in new sales capacity created.
- Existing sales of $775,000 retained.
- Inventories cut by more than $1.48 million.
- More than $1 million in cost savings (more than two-thirds of that in labor, the rest in overhead).

The focus on agility relates directly to a Northrop Grumman goal, to identify what the company calls best value suppliers.

What this means, in part, is that Northrop Grumman is developing balanced scorecards to evaluate particular groups of suppliers. For example, in looking at the suppliers for a particular product family, the company might evaluate the suppliers on 10 different criteria, price being only one. The others might be lead time, delivery, quality, the supplier's continuous improvement efforts, and so on.

Further, each score is weighted. With a particular product family, for example, Northrop Grumman might decide that lead time is especially important and count it as 20 percent of the total score. Each of the other criteria might be weighted to account for 15, 10 or even 5 percent. The supplier with the highest overall weighted score is most likely to win the contract.

Jordan stresses that Northrop Grumman does not require any supplier to take part in its lean supply chain management program.

However, he comments, "My expectation is that we're going to get the results either way. We are providing them with a potential tool kit. If they want to use the lean tools, that's great. We can help facilitate that. If they don't, if they want to use some other consulting group or some other approach, that's fine, but as part of our supplier management process, we have a scorecard, and we are expecting results one way or another. It's their call."

TAKEAWAYS

- Suppliers provide better service when they better understand their customers' business.
- The customer may need to provide incentives to involve the supplier.
- Close partnerships can lead to longer-term agreements, which benefit both parties.

10

Varied Approaches Help Make Supply Chain Initiatives Work

January, 2005

Your suppliers must be part of your lean strategy for you to achieve the greatest benefits. And making your supply chain lean involves diligence on your part, as well as use of a variety of tactics.

At dj Orthopedics, which began working with suppliers in 2002, those tactics include:

- Cutting by half the total number of suppliers

- Establishing kanban systems that transmit replenishment signals quickly

- Negotiating long-term agreements with suppliers to facilitate the kanban systems

- Arranging for the most geographically distant suppliers to ship materials on consignment

- Setting up vendor-managed-inventory systems with some suppliers

Perhaps most importantly, executives at the company worked hard to get to know their suppliers better than in the past. They visited supplier operations, learned as much as they could about them, explained what dj Orthopedics was trying to do, and in some cases worked with suppliers to help them become lean.

"That is all part of the whole program," comments Bill Holbrook, director of lean initiatives. "The better they understand your business, and the better knowledge you have of what their processes are, the more they're a partner in your business."

The supplier strategy, coupled with internal lean improvements, has proven valuable for dj Orthopedics. Inventory turns of both finished goods and raw materials have increased dramatically. And while executives do not reveal specific numbers, they say that cost savings achieved since 2002 amount to several million dollars, with the cost of goods sold down significantly.

Focus on Suppliers

At its headquarters plant in Vista, Calif., and a second facility in Tijuana, Mexico, dj Orthopedics makes products for the non-operative orthopedic and spine markets, including knee braces, pain management products and bone growth stimulation devices. Its more than 600 products produce annual sales of about $260 million, and the company employs more than 1,500 people worldwide.

Its lean initiatives began in 2001, spurred by problems the company faced in serving customers. At that time, dj Orthopedics typically had 15,000 units per day — or more than a day's worth of sales — on backorder. In addition, there were as many as 60 shortages of raw materials per day. That might not seem like much at a company that uses a total of perhaps 15,000 different raw materials, but the shortages typically occurred within the 200 to 300 materials used most often.

Holbrook, who had been a lean consultant, was brought into the company full-time to address the problems. He and Kevin Sumstine, the director of corporate purchasing and planning, became the leaders of the new strategy.

Initially, the focus was internal. Employees were educated about lean, more than 70 manufacturing cells were set up, and kaizen blitzes took place frequently.

"We had done a pretty good job internally. Backorders were coming down," Holbrook recalls. "But we really weren't going to make quantum leaps until we got the suppliers lined up."

One of the first priorities was to streamline the supply base. More than 450 companies supplied dj Orthopedics, and the company worked to reduce that to only about 200 today. Part of the strategy was to focus on companies located near the plants to reduce shipping time. Selection was also based on performance, and on whether suppliers were committed to quality and continuous improvement.

"We would say, 'let's take a look at your quality manual,'" Holbrook states. "If they say 'what's a quality manual?'... It was easy to reduce our supplier base when you ran into that."

Sumstine notes that the company offers help to suppliers. "We tried to show them some of our results. We offered up our services. It was up to them," he explains.

Holbrook adds, "In the first couple of years, I think we did 17 kaizen blitzes at supplier locations. That doesn't mean they were all successful. Sometimes we would go out and visit them, and we would end up a two- or three-day visit and say 'these guys are hopeless.'"

Kanban is the Key

One of the most significant aspects of the supplier strategy was to set up new systems for triggering replenishment of raw materials — what ultimately became the company's kanban system.

At about the same time dj Orthopedics was beginning its lean journey, the company was also installing a new ERP system from JD Edwards, which included an MRP module.

"We tried like heck to make MRP work," says Sumstine. "We eventually got to the point where we decided to unplug it. It wasn't a real popular decision. But that was really a turning point for us. We came to the realization that obviously kanban is a much simpler process and requires a lot less effort."

That's not to say the ERP system wasn't valuable. "One thing about JD Edwards, we could get at our raw material part numbers and past usage data pretty easily," Sumstine comments. "That allowed us to look at high-dollar raw materials and high-usage raw materials. We took that list and sorted it by supplier, and looked at the usage rates."

That data became the basis for a kanban system. The company felt that a three-card system would be best, meaning two standard quantities (for example, a bin or a pallet) would be by the operator while the third card would be awaiting delivery from the supplier. Each card represented daily usage times lead time, with the total multiplied by a safety factor of 1.5.

For example, suppose usage for a particular part was 100 per day, and the lead time to receive more parts was five days. Multiplying the two numbers produces a quantity of 500 parts. Multiplied by the safety factor of 1.5, the total would be 750. Therefore, one kanban card for that part would signal an order for 750 parts.

Initially, when a standard quantity was depleted, the kanban card would go back to the buyer who handled that part, and the buyer would call the supplier. Today, many of the replenishment signals are sent by e-mail.

A key factor in making the kanban system work was the establishment of long-term agreements with suppliers. The initial agreement sets up pricing terms, delivery terms, packaging configurations, and so on. Then each kanban signal simply releases parts or materials under that agreement, minimizing paperwork and approvals. This streamlines the process and makes suppliers more willing to negotiate price because of the quantities involved.

The company still has a few suppliers located far away from the plants. With those vendors, perhaps 30 percent of the total number of suppliers, dj Orthopedics has agreements under which materials are shipped on consignment, and stored either in company facilities or in a nearby warehouse. Once goods are issued from the storage location to the plant, storage personnel let the supplier know by e-mail, and an invoice is generated.

Low-dollar items — screws, washers, nuts and bolts — are supplied through vendor-managed-inventory agreements, under which vendor representatives visit the plants perhaps two times a week and replenish any items that are running low.

Looking Ahead

The progress made so far at dj Orthopedics is only the beginning. Holbrook says the company plans to reduce the number of suppliers further, probably by another 50 percent. And efforts are beginning to extend the initiatives down the supply chain as well as up.

"What this has taught us is that it was a progression," Holbrook explains. "It started internally, in the factory. That led us to work with our supply base to get them aboard. The next natural thing to try to do on the supply chain is go out and work with customers. It's how you deal with your customers, how you get your customers to buy your product. We're shipping them the product when they actually need it. We're getting closer to their actual demand. We're smoothing out the whole supply chain."

Sumstine notes that, in the past, some goods were being made in Mexico, shipped to the company's west coast distribution center, and then shipped to customers. Increasingly, the products are now being shipped directly to customers. "We really went from building inventory for these customers to building for demand," he states.

Meanwhile, internal lean initiatives are also expanding. As new products are designed, there is a greater focus on improving the design for manufacturability. The company has also begun lean initiatives in some office areas.

Holbrook and Sumstine's lessons learned from the experience so far are simple and straightforward. They include:

- Don't let anything interfere with real demand (a reference to MRP not meeting their needs).

- Accounting has to be a partner in a lean program.

- Simple is best (kanban vs. computer inventory system).

- Patience, but not complacency.

- Keep people in the loop.

- Communication is important throughout the value chain.

TAKEAWAYS

- Understanding your suppliers is the key to improving your supply chain.
- Reducing the number of suppliers reduces complexity.
- Contracts and procedures for transmitting information must be set up in advance.

Tatoos and Attitude Figure in Supply Chain Conversion

September, 2000

Not many companies can say that their customers tattoo the organization's name and logo on their bodies. Harley-Davidson is one of them, but the venerable Milwaukee motorcycle manufacturer doesn't take customer loyalty for granted. Harley must cut costs and get to market quicker just like everyone else. That means it can't take its supply chain for granted either.

Because Harley expanded its capacity in the late 1990s, suppliers were preparing to spend significant capital to increase their capacity. The challenge was to help suppliers expand capacity by eliminating waste instead of buying new equipment. So for the past few years Harley has been helping tier one, two, and even tier three suppliers implement lean.

Here's the framework of their methodology from Joe McDermond, process lead of the supplier continuous improvement team. McDermond is one of five members of the continuous improvement team, which is part of corporate purchasing.

Supply Chain Methodology

First, Harley selects suppliers that have good management attitudes toward improvement and have a significant dollar volume. The effort begins by explaining the program to a supplier's management in order to gain commitment. The supplier must agree to dedicate people and resources to the lean implementation.

Employees, including operators, are selected for a cross-functional continuous improvement team, which will make the shop-floor changes. It's important that the supplier appoint a team leader who is close to the plant floor but has the authority and ability to make decisions quickly.

Next, Harley CI personnel train supplier management and employees in fundamental lean principles and tools, including mapping, 5S, standard work, mistake-proofing, one-piece flow, TPM, and quick changeover.

They also perform a benchmarking study of the supplier's facility using data from the preceding three months to create a baseline record on downtime, pieces made per labor hour, rework percentage, scrap percentage, manpower levels, material yields, square footage of space used for production, travel distance, daily production vs. the schedule, setup time, on-time delivery, capacity, inventory and lead time. Savings from improvements are split 50-50 between Harley and the supplier.

Harley structures the actual shop-floor transformation as a three-month project rather than as a week-long kaizen workshop. A kaizen workshop won't work at a supplier that doesn't have an established continuous improvement mindset, warned McDermond. The workshop is "viewed as an event," he said. The supplier is apt to feel that Harley personnel were "here for a week, they're gone, we're rid of them."

After the three-month project, Harley CI people follow up with the supplier to help it develop a long-term conversion plan. The intent is to teach supplier CI people and employees how to perpetuate improvement activity.

Supplier participation in the program is voluntary, McDermond said, but there have been cases where participation has been "strongly recommended."

TAKEAWAYS

- A goal of supply chain improvements may be to increase capacity, not just cut costs.
- You can work best with suppliers who have a positive attitude toward improvement.
- Projects may take longer than the typical week-long kaizen event with suppliers that don't have an improvement mindset.

12

Challenge for Supplier Program Is Sustaining Lean Improvements

May, 2004

Rockwell Collins is helping its suppliers become lean. Midwest Metal Products, one of those suppliers, appreciates the help. But it's taken a while to find an approach that works.

The first project involving both companies was in 2000, when a Rockwell consultant helped create a "hot job" cell at Midwest, meaning a cell that worked on products with short lead times. "There was no follow-up by Rockwell, nor did we follow up like we should have," recalls Kevin Urban, president of Midwest. "We went back to our old ways."

A couple of other projects have occurred since then with better results, including one that successfully reduced the time needed to get customer orders ready for production.

However, Urban believes the best results may come from a new strategy: a year-long effort Rockwell has just launched with Midwest and four other suppliers, with monthly improvement projects and regular meetings.

This, Urban believes, will make it possible to sustain the changes being implemented, which is the reason he volunteered his company for it. "This program helps to culturize it and not let you drop it," he states.

Beyond making Midwest leaner, the assistance from Rockwell also helps build a relationship between the two companies – while simultaneously making Midwest less dependent on Rockwell.

On the one hand, Urban says, the new, year-long approach "puts us in touch with them more. It gets us involved in more areas of their business, so we can effect change going forward."

At the same time, "they want to make us and Rockwell less dependent on each other," notes Urban, whose Cedar Rapids, Iowa, company supplies Rockwell with precision fabricated metal products. "If there's an economic downturn, the suppliers will be healthy. I have no doubt it will improve our bottom line and improve our profits with Rockwell so we can be a supplier to them 30 years from now."

Rockwell Collins currently accounts for about 23 percent of Midwest's business, Urban says, adding that some of Rockwell's suppliers rely on it for more than half of their business.

Tim Taylor, senior advanced quality systems manager for Rockwell Collins, says the external suppliers the company has worked with so far (only a few, as the supplier program is in the early stages) have been very receptive to learning about lean.

"Suppliers in general are under a lot more pressure today to perform to a higher standard," he notes. "When we worked with these, they seemed almost hungry for the knowledge, hungry for the tools, hungry for a system that would allow them to meet our needs with less effort."

Urban agrees, explaining one reason for that hunger: "We know that they're going to end up going to Mexico and China if we don't get competitive."

Keys to a Relationship

A focus on suppliers is a relatively new part of a variety of lean initiatives at Rockwell Collins, which makes aviation and aerospace advanced communication, navigation and surveillance electronics for government and private industry. This focus began only within the last five years, and the majority of the effort so far has been on internal suppliers, Taylor says.

However, targeting suppliers is a natural outgrowth of lean initiatives, he adds. "Who are our best suppliers vs. our worst suppliers?" he asks. "From our data, it's easy to tell. Some have an enormous quantity of defects. Our approach allowed us to start looking at not only quality metrics, but cost. How is their on-time delivery – the things that make our business run very smoothly? It become obvious who the suppliers were we need to work with."

He adds, "We definitely have opportunities, to put it mildly. I have a supply base in the thousands. It's basically prioritizing those suppliers that impact you the most. I move down the Pareto chart to the next supplier that is causing us impact. We could definitely be busy for a while addressing both internal and external supplier issues. The key is the prioritization, the key to maintaining focus on what we call the big hitters."

Rockwell Collins uses a variety of methods in working with suppliers, from value stream mapping to brief, kaizen-like events called "lean bursts." Initial efforts have focused largely on improving flow, Taylor says, though he expects more of a focus on cost in the future.

His key points for a successful supplier program are not much different from the key points for any lean program: Address "social issues" as well as process issues, ensure management support, tie goals to business metrics, and so on. He also says it is important to require "cadence" reviews to maintain focus.

Urban stresses that "open, honest communication from both sides" is the most important element in making the relationship work.

And he adds that each side must recognize the other's needs. "The big thing coming up is Rockwell's acceptance that we must be profitable as we go forward," Urban says.

TAKEAWAYS

- Efforts to work with suppliers do not always go smoothly at the outset.
- Building relationships and achieving improvements takes time.
- "Social Issues" must be addressed as well as supply chain issues.

13

Improving Customers Creates Partners

March, 2005

Helping your customers apply lean and six sigma to improve their processes can strengthen your relationships with them and give you a competitive advantage.

That's what executives say at Xerox, which in 2003 made help with lean and six sigma part of the services it offers to customers.

"We've really become strategic partners (with customers)," says Rajiv Agarwala, vice president, lean six sigma deployment, for Xerox Global Services. "Whenever you go in and do an approach like this, at the end of the approach, you just have a completely different relationship with that customer. They truly consider you their partner. It's never about price anymore. It's about price and value, and that's a really good way to do business. We always like to be in that position."

The Xerox decision to focus on customers this way is an outgrowth of its own internal applications of lean and six sigma.

Application of six sigma began at Xerox in 1998, and the company says that strategy enabled it to reduce inventory levels by more than $880 million within 14 months. The approach was expanded beyond manufacturing in 2001 to include office processes. One result was that, a year later, the company's accounts receiv-

Gains in Sheriff's Department Are No Accident

Sheriff's deputies in Monroe County, N.Y., are spending significantly less time handling accident reports, and the department is spending significantly less money on the reports, thanks to help from Xerox.

The company spent much of 2004 working with the 1,200-employee department, which serves the area in and around Rochester, N.Y., wrapping up the project in the fall.

The focus of the effort was on the department's central records division, with the primary focus on accident reports, according to Cpl. John Helfer, the department's public information officer. Central records serves not only the department but also many local law enforcement agencies; the sheriff's department maintains the central database of all criminal records for the county.

But the operation was in need of improvement, as evidenced by a backlog of more than 3,000 records and more than four months of data entry, before the project began.

The application of lean and six sigma methods helped streamline the process; several steps were eliminated.

Improved use of information technology also contributed significantly to making the process better. A major step was the creation of a Web-based document access system. That new system is not yet

able balance was reduced by $117 million, and bad debt was down by 20 percent.

About two to three years ago, Agarwala says, the company shifted to an improvement approach combining both six sigma and lean. Lean approaches had been in use for a while, he notes, but independently of six sigma efforts. Working with the George Group consulting firm, those independent strategies were integrated into one.

Today, a strategy of continuous improvement is a part of how Xerox operates. Its 57,000 employees now include 27 full-time deployment managers, 500 active black belts, 2,000 senior executives who have completed leadership workshops, 1,700 active green belts, and 17,000 workers in yellow belt training.

at the point where individuals can access it. However, several insurance companies have contracts with the department so that they can directly obtain reports, eliminating the need for department personnel to be involved. Existing computer systems were integrated, and the overall accident report process has been digitized and streamlined.

The benefits resulting from the project include:

- Reducing the cost of processing an accident report from $28 to $8, for a savings of $500,000 annually.
- Reducing the cycle time from as much as three weeks to less than three days.
- Reducing the time spent by deputies on accident reports from 30 minutes to five minutes.

In addition, the department is now charging for accident reports, creating a revenue stream worth $32,000 per year.

Helfer says the department has not continued its relationship with Xerox at this point, although "we are always looking at plans to improve." He also notes that several local law enforcement agencies in the area "expressed interest in the kind of work done here."

He comments, "It's a benefit to sit down with another organization that was really able to define and understand our process. We were very pleased."

And while belt designations are typically associated with six sigma, Agarwala notes that the six sigma belt training at Xerox also includes lean training.

Goals and Mapping

However, the newest improvement direction at Xerox involves helping its customers. Xerox had already begun to use improvement approaches to help some customers with whom it had existing relationships. In 2003, the company adopted a formal strategy of using its lean/six sigma skills as a selling tool.

Today the company has more than 140 projects focused on external customers, and "without these programs our ability for continuous improvement, or the ability to add real high-level strategic value to our clients would be greatly diminished," according to Agarwala.

A consulting engagement with a customer typically begins with Xerox asking the customer to define its goal — what would make the engagement a success. That goal might be to reduce a backlog of paperwork, or to reduce expenses for a particular office process and/or make that process more efficient.

Another key step is assigning responsibilities for all aspects of the effort and determining who is accountable for what.

Xerox typically charges for this kind of consulting service, though exceptions might be made for long-time customers, Agarwala says. However, savings to be achieved might be part of the plan. When the situation is one that Xerox has encountered many times before, "if we do due diligence, we can almost tell them, 'we can identify a 20 percent opportunity for you,'" he explains.

"We lead with lean," he adds. Starting with lean tools is usually better than starting with six sigma approaches, Agarwala explains, because six sigma methods often require substantial data about the situation being studied, and "in most of the areas we work with, the customer does not have large amounts of data that define the process. Nobody's willing to invest that kind of time (to collect the data)."

However, he adds that once lean tools have been applied, "we understand where the breaks are, and then we set up a data collection plan around those broken areas. By then, you've already given the customer something. Now they are very interested in doing that (collecting data). They're excited about the opportunity."

Perhaps the most important lean tool used in the Xerox approach is value stream mapping.

"We are in the document management space," Agarwala states. "Our expertise lies in smarter document management. We have applied lean six sigma to that space. In a traditional lean approach, if you are looking at a manufacturing process, you follow a part through that process. In the document management space, we follow the documents. If someone asks us to go fix records management, we look at the documents. We follow them through from start to finish."

When the current state of the process is clearly identified, then other lean and six sigma tools can be applied to achieve actual improvements.

The Best and Brightest

Agarwala says consulting services at Xerox, including assistance with lean six sigma, are "definitely becoming a significant part of our business," although Xerox will not discuss specific sales figures. In some cases, the improvement focus is used to help acquire new clients; in other cases, it may be offered as a service to existing clients.

For other companies that may consider a similar approach with customers, Agarwala advises they "make sure you have your best and brightest people on it. Leadership attributes are more important than the technical attributes. You need to have a very strong element of leadership and customer facing. Start small and capitalize on your successes. Start with maybe two customers. Pick the customers whom you have the best relationship with, and do everything to make sure that engagement is successful."

He says that since starting this approach with customers, there have been no surprises and no negative feedback, except that "customers sometimes tell us, 'where the hell were you two years ago?' Every day we do this more and more, we get it reinforced that this is actually the right thing to do."

TAKEAWAYS

- Improvement services offered to customers should be an outgrowth of improvement methods applied internally.
- Customer goals, meaning what would make an engagement successful, must be determined before consulting begins.
- Lean methods should be applied before six sigma methods because many customers are not ready to collect the data needed for six sigma projects.

14

Coping With Variability is Key To Improving Retail Processes

July, 2005

Eliminating variability is impossible in retailing, where customers can walk in the door at any time. But retail processes can still be improved by finding effective methods to cope with variability.

That's a lesson that Trek Bicycle, a manufacturer, is teaching to the independent bicycle retailers who are its customers. Moreover, Trek is helping its dealers apply the appropriate methods so they can become more efficient — and sell more bicycles.

One of the challenges facing bicycle dealers is that they don't just sell bicycles, they also repair them. And since many dealers are small, with only a limited staff, an employee who is repairing a bike typically has to stop the repair work and act as a salesperson when a customer comes in.

"One of the things I've learned about working in the retail world is you can't tell your customers to follow your rules," says Jeff Amundson, Trek's director of continuous improvement. "All process controls stop when you get to the retail world. People come in. You can't tell them to make an appointment; they just come in. If you don't have a system, those people coming in the door are always going to bump service work."

Three "Buckets" Improve Work FLow

The key to improving operations at a bicycle store with a repair operation is to set aside time periods for specific jobs — and make sure that any given employee does only one job during a given period.

"Dealers were trying to get their employees to multi-task, and multi-tasking killed them," says Jessica Nguyen, continuous improvement specialist for Trek Bicycle.

Nguyen began working with Trek's dealers to help them become more efficient because "they were losing their shirts" on repair operations, which typically account for half their business, she explains.

Because dealers might not be familiar with term "time slicing," a concept of quick-response manufacturing, Nguyen called the method she developed the "3-Tier Defense" for dealer service centers. Its key elements are to identify three categories of work in the flow of bike repair: identify the skills, roles and responsibilities of each category, and focus on managing the mechanic's time to complete repairs.

The three categories or roles, which Nguyen calls buckets, are the service writer, who evaluates the bike brought in for repair and writes up the work order; the on-the-spot mechanic, who immediately performs any repairs that can be done in 15 minutes or less (such as adding flaps, making basic adjustments or installing a bell), and the repair mechanic, who handles bigger jobs.

One determination Nguyen made was that the job of service writer, which is typically done by less experienced personnel, should be handled by an experienced mechanic. That is so the job can be properly estimated at the outset, and the mechanic can make the

Trek is a member of the Center for Quick Response Manufacturing (QRM), located at the University of Wisconsin in Madison. The manufacturer's approach to dealing with the variability in a bicycle store involves a QRM concept known as time slicing.

This concept applies when there are conflicting demands on a shared resource. Time slicing may involve allocating blocks of time to cells (in manufacturing), or to teams or individuals, during which they have use of the resource. Trek's application of this con-

customer aware of unnoticed problems — for example, a customer might bring a bike in for brakes, and the mechanic could point out the bike also needs grips.

A small bicycle shop might have a staff of only three people — the owner, a salesperson and a mechanic. The busiest time of day might be from 3 p.m. to 7 p.m., when people typically bring bikes in for repair. Thus, the mechanic might be designated as the service writer during that afternoon period but would have 9 a.m. to 11 a.m. reserved for actually doing repairs. If a bike is brought in during the morning, the owner might act as service writer, leaving the mechanic's repair work undisturbed.

Bike shops often add temporary staff in the spring, their busiest season. A temporary employee might be trained to serve as the on-the-spot mechanic in the afternoon.

Nguyen notes that telling customers small repairs will be done in 15 minutes works well. "A customer will wait 15 minutes," she says. "During that time they are shopping in your store. They're a captive audience. They look at helmets, new bikes."

The results of adopting this system, says Nguyen, are "on average, we went from two to three weeks down to five to seven days, or about a 60 to 70 percent decrease in lead time. It worked really well."

In addition, she states, the system helps manage labor, builds teamwork and creates an environment for continuous improvement.

Nguyen says she has worked with about a dozen dealers so far. However, she notes that at a sales meeting last fall, she described Trek's approach to an audience of about 200 dealers and "almost 100 percent signed up for me to come out and help them."

cept to bicycle dealerships was developed by the company's continuous improvement specialist, Jessica Nguyen (see sidebar).

"It has to do with how people respond to that unpredictability of a customer walking through the door when you have already made a promise to fix that (other) customer's bike today," says Amundson. "Jessica worked out a system; by making sure everybody knows what their responsibilities are, nothing is totally ignored. Things are managed more carefully.

"I don't care what system you're talking about, every time you have a system that is trying to satisfy multiple customers or multiple demands, you end up with conflicts. You end up with someone saying 'I'm more important.' With time slicing, you say 'you are this important.' It assigns some levels of priorities, and you end up with all winners. Instead of making people stand in one long line, you make them stand in three short lines. It's the whole Toyota heijunka thing, making sure you do a little bit of everything all the time."

A Resource to Dealers

Trek, based in Waterloo, Wis., makes high-end bicycles. (Lance Armstrong rides a Trek.) They are sold by about 2,000 independent dealers in the United States, whose stores average about 4,000 square feet. There is also one company-owned store in Madison, Wis., which Amundson describes as a "concept store."

All bicycles are built to stock. Because of the value of the Trek brand, "people never ask us for a quote," Amundson claims, adding that the company never receives phone calls from dealers urgently asking for a particular model.

Trek began implementing kaizen methods internally in 1999 and had been a member of the QRM center for several years before that. After pursuing an improvement strategy internally, the company began making presentations at dealer shows about improvement strategies for dealers.

In some cases, the retailers seek help directly from Trek. In those situations, Amundson and others from the company act as consultants, working directly with the dealers. That has occurred so far with perhaps 20 to 40 dealers, he says. Other dealers hear the Trek presentations at sales meetings and implement improvement methods themselves. In addition, each Trek salesperson is required to help implement 5S methodology each year at two or three of his or her dealers. (Many dealers show interest in 5S, Amundson notes.)

In addition to improving repair processes, Trek helps dealers with other aspects of their business. "We've done a fair bit with order processing and receiving," he comments. "Dealers' processes sometimes are haphazard at best. They order things they don't need. They order twice."

Another problem area involves customers picking up bicycles after they have been repaired. Sometimes the dealer is stuck with a used bike because the customer simply doesn't pick it up. (That may not be true with a high-end Trek bike, but with other, less-expensive bikes dealers also repair.)

"The best solution we found to that problem was to shorten your lead time," declares Amundson. "They've tried phone calls, threats, pleasant reminders, they even consider delivering the bikes. The best absolute answer is make the lead time short. If you make an appointment for them to pick it up and do so at the minute they drop it off, they are more likely to pick up than if you say it will be done in a week or two."

Amundson observes, "we've had to be careful about the separation between sales and our continuous improvement consulting work. We are better able to do our work as consultants if we don't look at the brand name on the product that we're working on. If we're there to help a dealer, we've got to take his needs into consideration first before we consider what's best for Trek. We have to be committed to the idea that, if it's a strong dealer, that is good for Trek."

Trek is also interested in working at the other end of the supply chain, with its suppliers. However, that is difficult, he says, partly because Trek bicycles feature handlebars, saddles and tires that are brand-name products of other companies — meaning Trek does not have the option of going to another supplier for those parts.

"Supplier development here has to be completely different," Amundson says. "We do have plans. No doubt we're interested in it. We don't have a lot of good models we can follow right now. We're going to have to adopt and adapt."

TAKEAWAYS

* Committing people to specific tasks during specific periods helps cope with retail variability.
* Tasks (such as repairs) can be categorized by the amount of time they take.
* Consulting with customers should be separate from sales to customers.

Part III

Improving Distribution

OVERVIEW

Distribution is at the core of supply chain management. Developing strategy and building relationships with supply chain partners ultimately leads to efforts to streamline the flow of goods through distribution channels – the theme of the chapters in this section.

Amazon.com, a company renowned for its approach to retailing, needs a highly efficient warehouse to send thousands of items out to consumers every day. How it achieves this efficiency is described in Chapter 15.

General Motors Service Parts Operations ships items to dealers rather than consumers, but faces similar pressure to provide fast, accurate shipments. Chapter 16 explains how GM created a warehouse template of processes to reach its goals.

Chapter 17 describes how a shipper that works with GM, Menlo Logistics, developed a warehouse equivalent of takt time as the basis for improvement. Combined with a broader lean initiative and efforts to empower employees, the company has achieved sizable gains.

To help guard against errors in warehouse shipments, Chapter 18 – originally published as a Lean Advisor Q&A column – details specific steps that can be taken to error-proof distribution, from the standpoint of both suppliers and customers.

Another Q&A column, offered in Chapter 19, focuses on a very common, very practical problem – the use of returnable containers. Why they are part of a lean strategy and how to make it pay to use them is explained in this chapter.

Chapter 20 offers the perspective of a trucking company, Transfreight, that helps transport parts to Toyota from its suppliers. How a lean approach has changed logistics, and the importance of understanding that approach, are made clear.

A similar viewpoint is offered by another trucking company, Ryder. Chapter 21 explains how, in a lean world, Ryder sees its role very differently from that of the traditional trucking company.

15

Continuous Flow in the Warehouse

March, 2002

At a manufacturer, the person responsible for seeing that parts and materials flow smoothly through the production process might be the plant manager or production manager. At the Fernley, Nev., warehouse of Amazon.com, it's the flowmeister.

That term is affectionately applied to one person on each shift at the million-square-foot warehouse, one of five locations where Amazon's products are put together into orders.

The job is one aspect of a new set of processes – primarily better monitoring of flow – adopted by the company last fall to try to streamline the work required to complete orders

What occurs in the warehouse is not manufacturing, but it has a lot in common with manufacturing operations, or at least with assembly operations. Various parts (i.e., books, CDs, and numerous other items) are combined to create finished products (customer orders).

Much of what takes place in Fernley is handled by a $25 million sorting machine, but the process is not – and cannot be – totally automated. People must put items into the machine, and other people must put completed orders into boxes. Those boxes are then conveyed to shipping, where additional people work. The pace varies, along with staffing needs.

Millions of books, CDs and other items are stored in Amazon.com's Fernley, Nev., site as well as in its five other warehouses.

And like a manufacturer or assembler, Amazon.com wants to eliminate waste and mistakes from its process, reduce the time and staffing required to do the job, and lower costs.

To a large extent, the systems and procedures put in place in 2001 are helping to achieve those goals. During the 2001 holiday season – the busiest time of year for most retailers -- Amazon.com claims to have processed 37.9 million items through its 5 centers (a reported increase of 10 to 15 percent over the previous year) and claims to have completed 99 percent of all orders on time.

From a production standpoint, perhaps the most important fact is that all this was accomplished with 3,700 full time employees and about 4,000 temporary workers - a one-third reduction in staffing from the previous year.

That streamlining undoubtedly helped contribute to the fact that

Amazon.com workers transfer completed orders from the final conveyor system to shipping docks.

in fourth quarter 2001, the online pioneer reported its first-ever net profit in nearly seven years of operations.

It's All About Monitoring

Each day — actually, prior to each shift — managers review the orders they will have to fill and determine the staffing required, making last-minute adjustments if necessary to the number of staffers or where they are deployed.

According to Greg Hopkins, flow manager at the Fernley site, monitoring processes is the key to making the system work. Bar-code scanning permits real-time monitoring — Hopkins compares it to a heart-rate monitor — of product leaving the picking department.

"Once we've set up the daily schedule, we monitor processes. It allows us to see spikes. We have rates from one process to another.

We want the picking department to operate at a given rate," he says.

Software that was developed in-house is an important part of analyzing flow needs. "We actually had a flow team as part of the initial project," Hopkins notes. "It took about four months to come up with a working or functional specification, and within 30 days we had version one running." The warehouse is now on version three.

The program went live the last week of November - a critical time. "The thing we did learn is what we expected to get out of it," says Kirk Longo, senior operations manager for change management. "Will this help us with our constraint management during the peak season? The tool actually does work. Product doesn't flow to an upstream or downstream process with capacity we can't handle."

Hopkins is even more enthusiastic. "It's like a night-and-day comparison," he says. "The flow monitoring tools allowed us to be a lot more preventive rather than reactive."

Not surprisingly, Amazon's managers don't speak about lean manufacturing. But Longo does note that a variety of employees have backgrounds in manufacturing as well as distribution. "We understand constraints and constraint management," he comments. "We are learning the process here, and what the constraints are, how we can manage the constraints."

However, even more than constraint management, Longo and Hopkins talk about the customer and Amazon.com's goal of delivering orders when promised.

"We want to maintain the customer expectation," Hopkins says.

TAKEAWAYS

- Warehouse operations must be monitored constantly.
- Staffing requirements can change daily, depending on orders.
- The rates at which departments, such as picking, operate should be set in advance.

16

At GM, Parts Distribution Centers Can Be Lean, Too

October, 2001

General Motors has been applying the concepts of lean production to its parts distribution operations – and achieving significant gains as a result.

"We centered on implementing lean and common processes that would produce a measurable, positive impact," said Ronald West, general director of warehousing and distribution for General Motors Service Parts Operations (SPO).

Placing inbound unipacks of parts on a tilt table.

After an initial pilot project in 1998, the automaker learned that "in order to maximize delivery performance improvement or optimize the related savings, that smaller, less complicated facilities are more efficient," West said at a conference in 2001. The result was creation of a warehouse template of processes.

According to GM spokesperson Susan Reyes-Nothoff, the initial project took place at two plants: a brownfield parts distribution center (PDC) in Willow Run. Mich. and a greenfield site in Jacksonville, Fla. Since 1998, she said, productivity has increased

Moving inbound parts into designated locations.

by 43 percent at the Michigan location and 24 percent in Florida.

Since 1999, SPO has opened new PDCs in Charlotte, N.C., Jackson, Miss., Los Angeles, Memphis, Columbus, Ohio, Cincinnati and Martinsburg, W.Va. Additional PDCs are either planned or under construction in Fort Worth, Falls Township, Pa., and Chicago.

Reyes-Nothoff said the Charlotte facility has seen a gain of 113 percent, while performance at the Jackson site is 135 percent better than the old facility.

Sorting outbound bulk parts.

Overall, West said GM SPO has achieved significant improvements in delivery, responsiveness, quality, productivity and cost by redesigning the interior of its facilities and reshaping exterior relationships.

Those gains came from a strategy that West said initially involved a three-stage improvement of internal operations. First, "we had to improve our quality and responsiveness

Picking up orders from the dispatch board.

throughout our existing parts distribution centers," he said. "We looked at various metrics to track performance and set aggressive and measurable improvement targets."

Next came the competitive warehousing pilot, designed to evaluate best practices in existing PDCs – with the conclusion that smaller facilities are better.

Sorting picked parts into dealer holes.

Finally, SPO separated its AC Delco and GM Parts business into dedicated facilities. West said this helped improve SPO's customer focus by reducing the complexities of the AC Delco business – reducing order fragmentation and lead time, and improving availability and order response time.

After the internal changes, SPO partnered with Schneider Logistics to improve externally. The partners created a new solution that "modifies inbound material process, levels material flow, communicates schedules and priorities, monitors performance and tracking methods, and provides for further improvements," according to West.

The result, West said, is that "we have designed-in flexibility with the potential to grow as the business dictates. As our work force applies these new techniques and processes, we are solidifying our competitive position."

Distributing outbound parts in a dealer sortation lane.

SPO, headquartered in Grand Blanc, Mich., markets automotive replacement parts and accessories worldwide under the GM and AC Delco brand names. SPO also provides inventory consultation and recommendations for improvement in parts, accessories and service merchandising under the GM Goodwrench Service Plus banner.

TAKEAWAYS

- Smaller, less complicated facilities can be more efficient.
- A template of processes can be applied to each facility.
- A dedicated operation may be required for a large customer.

17

Warehouse Sets a Faster Pace

September, 2004

Takt time, which tells you how quickly your shop floor should be producing product, can also tell you how quickly product should be moving through your warehouse.

That concept is central to operations at Menlo Worldwide's Lean Logistics Center in Brownstown, Mich., which serves primarily as a distribution center for service parts going to General Motors dealers.

What the managers at the center call "takt time" is not calculated in exactly the same way as manufacturing takt time, but the concept is similar. Managers know how long it takes to put away the different types of parts received in a shipment, how many parts must be put away in a day, how rapidly the parts must be put away to get the work done, and what staffing level is required to achieve that (see sidebar, page 105).

The use of a form of takt time is part of a broader lean focus at the center, which began operations last fall. That focus includes a strong emphasis on employee empowerment and continuous improvement, plus somewhat less use of technology than other facilities.

"We've had an amazing response," boasts Greg Lehmkuhl, Menlo's director of automotive operations. "People felt like they were involved in the project. We've literally had $9-an-hour tem-

Employees at Menlo's Lean Logistics Center in Brownstown, Mich., follow a "takt time" that sets the pace for putting shipments away.

porary employees write our standard operating procedures from the first day. The hardest thing from a manager's standpoint is to allow the employees to really take this approach. We have to allow them to fail and struggle through the process."

Empowerment

The 171,000-square-foot Brownstown facility employs 29 people, contains more than 7,000 storage locations and handles about 5,000 part numbers. Most of its operations involve receiving parts from GM suppliers in Australia and Korea, then distributing them to GM dealers. About 30,000 square feet are used to provide similar services to Axle Alliance Company.

Like many suppliers of goods and services to automotive companies, Menlo found that "because our customer was so driven to lean, it really forced us to adopt this," Lehmkuhl admits.

However, the company is pleased with the results. In fact, while the lean approach is currently in place at only a handful of Menlo

"Takt Time" For a Warehouse

To calculate takt time in manufacturing, you divide available production time by the number of products to be made, which tells you the time available to make one product.

At Menlo Worldwide's Lean Logistics Center, a similar calculation occurs, as follows:

The table below shows an example of the work to be done in a given shift. In this case, parts are sorted into three categories, based on size. This sorting makes it possible to know how many parts can be away in 20 minutes.

The "X" numbers in the first column represent the commodity codes used to sort the products. The term "lines" refers to how many line items in a particular category must be put away.

Aisle Range	Lines	Put-away Quantity	Put-away Time	Shift Time
X27 – X36	300	10	20 min.	440 min.
X37 – X47	300	15	20 min.	
X48 – X53	760	20	20 min.	

The formula for calculating Put-away assignments is

$$\frac{\text{Lines}}{\text{Put-away Qty.}} = \text{Put-away assignments}$$

which in this case becomes

$$\frac{300}{10} + \frac{300}{15} + \frac{760}{20} = 88 \text{ Assignments}$$

Calculation of the Put-away Pace is

$$\frac{\text{Put-away}}{\text{Pace}} = \frac{\text{Shift Time (Minutes)}}{\text{Assignments}} = \frac{440}{88} = 5 \text{ minutes}$$

The required number of people is then calculated by dividing Put-away Time (20 minutes) by the Put-away Pace (5 minutes), which determines that four people are needed for this shift.

$$\text{People Required} = \frac{\text{Put-away Time}}{\text{Put-away Pace}} = \frac{20}{5} = 4$$

In Menlo's Lean Logistics Center, products of similar sizes are put away together, which standardizes put-away times.

facilities, it is being rolled out to all Menlo warehouses globally.

"Definitely the first and primary differentiator between the lean and non-lean facilities is employee empowerment," says Lehmkuhl. "One of the concepts is the team leader concept and autonomous work groups. These people were taken aback. They worked in other warehouses where they were generally told what to do. Right from the beginning, they really loved our approach. They were told right from the beginning they would have to understand the work, and understand what the value is they are driving for the customer."

The approach at Brownstown includes many standard lean tools and methods: visual controls, standardized work, error-proofing, kaizen events.

One of the more interesting side effects of adopting this approach is that the Brownstown facility uses information technology less than other Menlo sites. The center does have a warehouse management system (WMS), but Lehmkuhl notes that it is simpler than systems the company uses elsewhere, with greater reliance on manual, paper-based processes.

"We wanted to use a Toyota philosophy of building your process, then building the technology around the process," he explains. "We chose to go with a lower-end system because we wanted our employees to have more flexibility."

Menlo also offers what it calls an Incentive Compensation Plan, which, while not a lean method, is designed to drive good performance. Employees can receive points based on performance, with those points redeemable for various benefits. In addition, GM rewards Menlo for meeting certain thresholds of quality, damage and so on, and those provisions are tied into employee incentives. "For a manager, as much as 48 percent of his compensation derives from how well we get our metrics," says Lehmkuhl.

Commodity Codes

One technique at the heart of the center's lean approach is what Menlo calls commodity code sorting. As parts are received, they are sorted and put away according to their particular codes. These codes sort the parts by size, which "really helped drive standardized work," Lehmkuhl notes. "We can put say 30 parts (of a given size) on a cart. Then we know that in this area, we should be able to put away 30 parts in a 20-minute cycle. By sorting this way, we've been able to drive productivity. If a team leader is not back in 20 minutes, he's not performing to his goals."

The concept also applies when parts are being shipped out. For example, in some cases, Menlo packages parts in addition to shipping them, and "we know that every 20 minutes we should be able to package X amount of this product," he states.

The Brownstown facility is still in the early stages of its lean journey. Objectives for 2004 range from complete detail process mapping of all warehouse operations to having visual work measurement for all work areas.

For other companies considering applying lean principles to distribution operations, Lehmkuhl advises, "You have to truly engage the workforce. It's a philosophy and not an initiative. It cannot be the flavor of the week. It has to be truly a cultural and philosophical change in the organization, and if the company directors don't understand that, then you're wasting your time."

TAKEAWAYS

- A warehouse should have a set work pace.
- Lean concepts apply to distribution.
- Employee empowerment is key.

18

Error-Proofing Warehouse Picking

Sam Becktel
April, 2005

Some of our customers claim they are not getting everything they ordered. How can we error-proof warehouse picking and shipping?

The key to reducing this defect is to first recognize that it can be caused by either of two types of errors:

- The part was not shipped, but should have been – a supplier error.

- The part was shipped, but the customer did not recognize that they got it – a customer error.

There are ways to eliminate both types of errors.

Supplier Errors

1. Do your picking and shipping people KNOW that the customers think they are getting shorted? Simply getting your people to understand the issue and begin to kaizen the process is a great place to start.

2. How well would your stockroom, picking and shipping areas stand up to a 5S evaluation? If the workplace is not orderly, what goes into the shipment cannot be orderly.

3. Consider pre-packing and sealing commonly requested kits of small parts (e.g., screws, nuts and bolts). Weighing the bag is a simple and effective error-proofing technique to make sure the right parts are in it before it goes into stock.

4. Review part-marking and identification schemes. It should be easy to identify and pick up the right part. If you have right and left, or top and bottom, versions of a part, use templates or other visual devices to verify which it is.

5. Use common totes or boxes for picking, with the pick list visible on the box. (Clear paper-holders work fine). It should be easy to look at a shipment and see which parts have been picked and which have not.

6. Consider whether it makes sense to design totes specifically for your application. For example, some totes have dividers to form 12 internal bins, which are numbered. Each item goes into its own bin. It is then easy to see how many items have been picked and compare that to the pick list. Parts too big for the bin go into their own tote, and a token is placed in the bin to show that the part was picked.

Customer errors

1. Review part-marking and identification schemes from the customer's point of view. You might know exactly what a W32-29-Q-Rev 6 is, but the customer may only know he needs a "small green valve." The part tag may need wording on it.

2. Does your shipping/packing/billing documentation include information the customer needs? Many documentation schemes are set up to make sure that invoices match receiving documents. In the worst example I have seen, the shipping documentation only included the customer's purchase order information and the total amount due. There was no way for the customer to determine what was supposed to be in the box. As a result, many customers would simply put

the box into the "exception" pile and call the purchasing agent to sort it out. This increased the opportunity for errors as boxes were sometimes opened, left unattended or rifled through by desperate manufacturing people on scavenger hunts.

3. If there is a problem or question, does the shipment make clear how to contact the right person in your organization to resolve the issue?

4. Do you have just a few customers that are the source of many complaints? If so, "ride" a box through your shipping and their receiving/payment process. You may be astounded at what you find. By doing this once, I discovered that a large customer had revamped their tracking system to include a bar coding scheme – but had forgotten to notify us. Every shipment we made to them (about 50 a day) became an "exception."

5. Take a digital photo of the parts for each shipment just before they go into the box. Two things happen. First, packing and shipping people realize the importance of accuracy. Second, the "I didn't get this part" complaints are handled by providing a copy of the photograph showing the part really was there. Customers go back and look a second time, and the part is found. In one case I am familiar with, simply taking these photographs reduced "real" customer short shipment complaints by 80 percent in 60 days.

TAKEAWAYS

- Both you and your customers commit errors, and they are not the same.
- Your (supplier) errors may involve organization, flow of information and handling equipment and boxes.
- Many customer errors involve not having information to verify what is in a shipment.

19

Lean Leads to Returnable Containers

Michel Baudin
November, 2003

As part of their lean conversion, our customers are demanding that we ship parts in returnable containers. How should we respond?

Agreeing is advisable, but you should also understand why they are doing it and how you can make it work to your advantage. Returnable containers protect parts better than disposables, their dunnage (packing material) mistake-proofs your shipping, they are cheaper if used long enough and frequently enough, and they are friendlier to the environment. In addition, when used exclusively for an item, they cap inventory, and can sometimes serve as pull signals.

The closest non-lean manufacturers get to reusing packages is recycling materials. Lean manufacturers, on the other hand, favor returnables, which dominate in Toyota's supply chain, even for overseas shipments. In other industries, one sees plants where suppliers' disposable containers do not make it past Receiving, and where parts are transferred to returnable bins at the point of entry.

In terms of quantifiable advantages of returnable containers, users emphasize the following:

- Packaging quality: Plastic containers, particularly stackables with part-specific dunnage, are simply better protection against mechanical, chemical, or electromagnetic damage than corrugated cardboard boxes. This is best measured on a pilot implementation, and the results can then be extrapolated.

- Costs: While switching to returnables eliminates some activities, it requires others, and we cannot say that the cost of handling returnables is always lower than that of disposables. While disposables have to be bought, stored and erected at the supplier side, and destroyed at the customer side, returnables have to be sorted, shipped back, handled with care, and tracked. In milk runs to local suppliers, returning containers fill up trucks that would otherwise travel empty. For overseas shipments, collapsibles share space with return freight in ocean-going containers.

  The operational costs, however, are small compared to the costs of the containers themselves. If one cardboard box costs $2 and a returnable $40, then the returnables become cheaper once they have been used more than 20 times. The number of times a returnable container can be used is key, but so is its frequency of use. The payback period on our $40 returnable container is 20 years if used once a year, but 4 weeks if used daily. Household coffee makers are sold to consumers in disposable packages because they don't buy one every day. A car assembly line, on the other hand, uses 1,000 sets of rear view mirrors every day.

- Environmental responsibility: Some managements view the switch to returnable containers as a way of "greening" the company. The public relations benefits of this may be substantial and need to be assessed by Marketing.

Necessary Conditions

The conditions for making returnable containers pay are therefore as follows:

1. Handle them with care to maximize the number of uses.

2. Use them only for items with steady demand.

3. Keep their numbers low enough for them to rotate frequently between customer and supplier.

4. Take advantage of available transportation.

The two-bin system is the ancestor of the kanban system, and the opportunity to use returnable containers as pull signals immediately comes to mind. It is sometimes possible, keeping in mind the following limitations:

- Containers used as pull signals must be dedicated not only to an item, but to a pull-loop on this item. The same container cannot be used through multiple operations.

- As signals, empty containers cannot travel faster than the vehicles they are on. While hardcopy kanbans have the same limitations, e-kanbans and fax signals don't.

- Containers cannot be placed in collection boxes or pinned on boards, which limits the possible processing of the information they carry.

Returnable container ownership can be on the customer or the supplier side, or shared between the two in arrangements that motivate both sides to make them work. Container maintenance and replacement is usually a supplier duty. Customers, on the other hand, are responsible for ensuring that the same containers are used for delivery of the same item to multiple sites.

On the customer side, containers designed for transportation are not always fit for part presentation in production, and disposables cannot be completely eliminated because they remain the norm for shipping finished goods for distribution to consumers. On the supplier side, dealing with different customer-specific style of returnables is an additional challenge, requiring suppliers to have their own tracking system, involving both visible management and computers.

TAKEAWAYS

- Returnable containers are more prevalent in lean operations because they provide better protection, mistake-proofing and lower costs.
- These containers should only be used for items with steady demand, and should be rotated frequently.
- These containers may function as kanban pull signals.

Lean Philosophy Drives Trucking Company

April, 2001

In an ideal just-in-time world, a plant with 200 suppliers would receive a half-hour's worth of production every hour on trailer trucks carrying a mix of parts from every supplier. In reality, particularly the North American reality of vast distances between customers and suppliers, "that's not possible," said Robert Martichenko, general manager of logistics development for Transfreight LLC. "However, we can get it to the point where we have 30, 40, or 50 suppliers on trailers and it represents an hour of production."

Headquartered in Cambridge, Ontario and Erlanger, Kentucky, Transfreight is a third-party logistics company, specializing in lean inbound logistics techniques, including transportation and route design. They are responsible for providing logistics among all Toyota's North American plants and suppliers. At Fall 2000's Productivity Conference on Lean Management, he explained how their lean logistics system operates in a very different environment than in Japan. Not only are the distances greater here, but there is no captive supply base dedicated to one big customer.

"Yes, we got a lot of trucks and a lot of trailers, *but understanding the philosophy of why we are doing things the way we are is so important to our organization*," he said. "We follow the Toyota Production System standards and principles to a 'T' within our company." That means lots of standardized work, kaizen, and teamwork.

The "number 1 rule of the game" in lean logistics is frequency of daily deliveries, said Martichenko. "Your frequency has to be high." Frequent deliveries support small lot production and its attendant benefits of restraining overproduction, quick response to market shifts, and early detection of quality problems, among others. It also saves space. If a plant with one shift needs 500 square feet to store 2,000 parts delivered once per day, it has 500 square feet "sitting there empty waiting for tomorrow morning at 8 a.m. when the truck shows up again," he noted.

Such a delivery schedule is not unlike milk runs, which are often used in the initial stages of JIT. A truck driver driving a timed route to several suppliers "picks up what we need," said Martichenko. Typically, the truck would pick up at vendor A, then vendor B, then vendor C to get one day's requirement for a customer. The problem with such a schedule is that the truck usually arrives in the morning with a whole day's worth of parts. "You still have the problem of where are the parts going to go" inside the customer's plant. And quality problems might be obscured by the lot size, which will be larger than lots delivered more often.

The situation improves if trucks deliver twice daily. Martichenko noted that a truck could arrive at 8 a.m. with only 1,000 parts, which are used by 12 p.m. when another truck arrives with 1,000 parts. "Now, our square footage requirement is only 250 feet." Four deliveries per day drop it to 125 square feet.

"We have suppliers who deliver right now to our customers as much as 16 times per day," he said. "One of our trucks is pulling out of their facility and another one is pulling in. Our drivers quite literally wave to each other."

Cross Docks

But achieving frequent deliveries is not easy. "If you have huge volumes it's easy to design frequent runs," Martichenko noted.

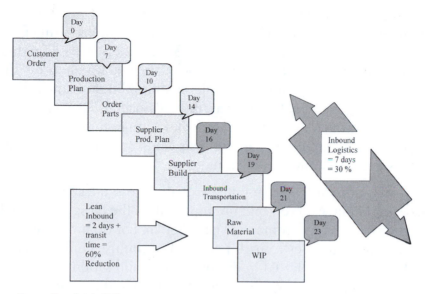

Source: Transfreight LLC

The example above assumes a company is building to order not to stock. If the inbound logistics from a supplier takes seven days, that's 30 percent of the process to the start of manufacturing. Robert Martichenko of Transfreight says that a lean logistics effort should be able to cut inbound logistics to little more than two days for a 60 percent reduction.

"We're not suggesting that if the current transportation budget is four or five percent of sales, all of a sudden you can go to 12 percent." You must consider volume along with distance and geography. "You must look at where suppliers are in relation to each other and in relation to the customer," he said.

What you often find are many low-volume suppliers. In such cases, it doesn't make sense to schedule 16 shipments daily for a supplier shipping just 16 containers, especially if you also have a supply base scattered across a wide geographic area. *The solution is a cross dock, a facility where shipments from many suppliers can be consolidated* and sent to the customer in frequent intervals. From the cross dock, trucks can run directly to the plant every 1.5 hours, 12x per day.

Inside the cross dock, the collection routes come in with "three, four, five, six, or more suppliers on them," explained Martichenko. At regular intervals, the mixed loads go to the manufacturing facilities in exactly the quantities needed to meet their leveled production requirements. "These cross docks are not warehouses," he noted. Cross docks supply multiple facilities, but are small. Parts sitting in them can get in the way, or be damaged. "We have a target that parts don't stay in a cross dock for more than six hours. If something is sitting for more than six hours, we put the plan-do-check-act kaizen procedure on it."

Consolidating supplier shipments at the cross dock creates frequency, but how do you split up shipments to the cross dock? Look at your lot sizes, recommends Martichenko. For example, say your customer's plant uses 75 parts per day. But you use containers that hold a minimum of 50. On day one, you could send two lot sizes of 50 parts each to the customer. On day two, the customer will order one because it has 25 left from day one. On day three, the customer will order two lots again.

"If there isn't good communication between the customer and the supplier, the supplier never knows why this is happening," Martichenko said. "The next thing you know the supplier says, Some days they order two lots, so we better have three in stock at all times just in case." The result is excess inventory. The situation can be greatly improved if the supplier agrees to change the packaging so it can ship 25 pieces per tote. Now the customer can order three lots every day.

In designing routes, Transfreight engineers aim to use trailer space efficiently. Engineers must consider which suppliers can stack containers with those used by other suppliers. Suppliers must reuse the same packaging. They can't use a steel rack one day and a container the next or drivers will have damaged parts or "cube outs" – no room when they arrive at the last suppliers on their routes. "There's no way we could do our job without 100 percent returnable packaging," Martichenko said.

Transfreight customers have "zero receiving functions,"

Martichenko said. Drivers verify the parts. When they enter the supplier's facility, "they know exactly what they have to pick up. If it's not there in the right quantity and the right packaging, they call the office." The customer is notified and the driver doesn't leave until "we figured out why what they are supposed to pick up isn't there."

Level Deliveries

In addition to frequent deliveries, and efficient trailer utilization, lean logistics also must consider the rate at which to send shipments to the customer. The goal, as inside the plant, is to create a level flow. *If trucks arrive at various intervals, the plant can't meet its target inventory levels.* For instance, let's say a trailer from the cross dock carrying parts from 30, 40 or 50 suppliers arrives at the plant stores area at 8 a.m. and is quickly sent to the line. In two hours, if the plant is looking for more parts, another trailer must arrive. And in two hours, another must arrive. Without leveling, the customer's plant risks running out of parts or having too many.

If a trailer is inbound every two hours, one must be outbound from the customer's site every two hours. Suppliers are counting on the truck to bring back the returnable packaging. "In a lean environment, they don't allow you to have excess packaging," said Martichenko. If the truck is late returning the packaging, the suppliers will have parts but no containers.

Another factor to monitor in a lean logistics system is how long trailers "sleep" or wait to be unloaded at the customer plant. Transfreight's most distant supplier is 60 hours from the plant; it can't "sleep" for more than eight hours.

Visibility is becoming more important in logistics. Visibility in a lean system doesn't mean warehouse management systems but "knowing where the freight is," said Martichenko. "A day doesn't go by when we don't get a phone call asking about part number such-and-such, where is it, what road is it on." A lean logistics provider must know when and how many parts are coming in off a route, when they will hit a cross dock, and when the shipments will hit the plant.

Knowing the locations of parts is critical, especially during bad weather, because you can reroute trucks around the storm. Or if a parts shortage is looming for a customer, you can identify where the next truck is with the needed parts. "You may not have more than four or five hours of inventory at the facility at any given time, so what's in transit is quite literally your safety stock. It's quite important to know where it is."

To know where everything is, Transfreight doesn't manage by trailer numbers. "We have no idea what the trailer numbers are," said Martichenko. "We manage everything by the routes and the parts. It's a fundamental shift. Our mindset is that we are not running trucks and trailers. We're running auto parts, and we just happen to use trucks and trailers to do that."

Logistics is evolving from the traditional model, which was often led by purchasing's goal to get volume discounts from suppliers offering great deals. "When we were calculating how good a deal it was, *we didn't figure out that we had to get another 100,000 square feet of warehouse space to store the parts*," noted Martichenko. The batch method of logistics also created dock congestion at plants.

Martichenko cited industry statistics showing that 60 percent of the $921 billion logistics industry is transportation costs. Of that, 36 percent is calculated as inventory carrying costs. You can disagree over the exact method of calculating inventory, "however, it's a huge number, and I think everybody will say it has to be reduced," he said.

TAKEAWAYS

- Lean logistics requires frequent deliveries.
- Cross docks make sense when you have many low-volume suppliers.
- Level deliveries are essential, as is visibility of information.

For a Trucking Company, It's Not About Trucks Anymore

September, 2002

The primary role of trucking companies serving automakers is no longer just to move things from here to there. It's helping their customers manage logistics operations — and that has a lot to do with the evolution and growth of lean principles.

That's the view of Tom Jones, senior vice president for Ryder, in charge of global automotive, aerospace and industrial supply chain solutions.

"Customers are seeing tremendous value in intellectual capital," Jones says. "They're turning to us not because we have a lot of trucks and drivers, but because we have a very deep set of knowledge about how to run these systems.

"We're going to be continuing to move to a supply chain manager role or a lead logistics role. In contrast to where we started in the 1980s, these services then were really just kind of a throw-in. Now it's a total reversal. Trucks and drivers are commoditized. They're not as important to the customer as the knowledge."

Ryder announced a deal to develop and facilitate a just-in-time system for delivery of inbound supplies to Honda's plant in Lincoln, Ala. The agreement comes three years after Ryder began doing similar work for Honda's facility in Alliston, Ontario. The Alabama effort will focus on maximizing use of trailer load space, optimizing routes to reduce the number of miles, and maximizing use of lean levels of trucks, trailers and other equipment.

Jones sees a shift from the 1980s. At that time and into the early '90s, he says, the JIT concept "was very immature. JIT in the early '90s was to have no warehouses. Everything moved on a dedicated truck at a dedicated time for pickup and delivery into a single, specific assembly plant." In addition, he said, part of the early concept was "to do whatever it takes to make sure the assembly plant is running efficiently; taking care of cost (of logistics) was an afterthought." Today, he says, cost is a much greater consideration.

As the number of auto plants grew, the dedicated system proved to be inefficient and costly, Jones comments. Meanwhile, the number of tier one suppliers dropped significantly through consolidation, and manufacturers were outsourcing subassembly work to a much greater degree. Automakers have therefore moved to having a trucking company "making pickups at multiple (supplier) plants, taking them to a deconsolidation center, and reshipping to assembly plants."

And in 2002, the trend has seen a new twist: Ryder has become a "quasi-tier-one supplier," Jones says, where "we've actually progressed to the point where we are doing some relatively minor subassembly."

Overall, "there's tremendous growth out there," he concludes. "It's still a very vibrant market. JIT is not going away. It's the way to do business. No one is retreating from it."

TAKEAWAYS

- Trucking companies now manage logistics operations rather than just make shipments.
- The change is the result of maturation of the JIT concept since the 1980s.
- Some trucking companies also perform assembly.

Citations

(All articles taken from the *Lean Manufacturing Advisor*)

Chapter 1: "Expanding an Initiative Beyond Your Enterprise." November 2002: Volume 4, Number 6

Chapter 2: "Reducing Supply Chain Complexity." April 2002: Volume 3, Number 11

Chapter 3: "In a Race Against Time, adidas Leaps Forward." October 2002: Volume 4, Number 5

Chapter 4: "A New Paradigm Supports U.S. Troops." September 2002: Volume 4, Number 4

Chapter 5: "Report: Lean Afghan Logistics Were Better Than Desert Storm." June 2004: Volume 6, Number 1

Chapter 6: "Customers—and Suppliers—Offer Tips for Working with Suppliers." June 2001: Volume 3, Number 1

Chapter 7: "4 Steps for Deploying Lean 'Blueprint' Through the Supply Chain." April 2000: Volume 1, Number 11

Chapter 8: "A New Metric Measures Suppliers." July 2005: Volume 7, Number 2

Chapter 9: "Lean Supply Chain Effort Is Built on Research, Planning & Structure." June 2005: Volume 7, Number 1

Chapter 10: "Varied Approaches Help Make Supply Chain Initiatives Work." January 2005: Volume 6, Number 8

Chapter 11: "Tatoos and Attitude Figure in Supply Chain Conversion." September 2000: Volume 2, Number 4

Chapter 12: "Challenge for Supplier Program is Sustaining Lean Improvements." May 2004: Volume 5, Number 12

Chapter 13: "Improving Customers Creates Partners." March 2005: Volume 6, Number 10

Chapter 14: "Coping With Variability is Key To Improving Retail Processes." July 2005: Volume 7, Number 2

Chapter 15: "Continuous Flow iin the Warehouse." March 2002: Volume 3, Number 10

Chapter 16: "At GM, Parts Distribution Centers Can Be Lean, Too." October 2001: Volume 3, Number 5

Chapter 17: "Warehouse Sets a Faster Pace." September 2004: Volume 6, Number 4

Chapter 18: "Error-Proofing Warehouse Picking." April 2005: Volume 6, Number 11

Chapter 19: "Lean Leads to Returnable Containers." November 2003: Volume 5, Number 6

Chapter 20: "Lean Philosophy Drives Trucking Company." April 2001: Volume 2, Number 11

Chapter 21: "For a Trucking Company, It's Not About Trucks Anymore." September 2002: Volume 4, Number 4

Index